A QUEST FOR MEANING
A Memoir from Pit to Pulpit; from Business to Philanthropy

By
John M Hayes

A QUEST FOR MEANING: A Memoir from Pit to Pulpit; from Business to Philanthropy

Author: John M Hayes

Copyright © 2025 John M Hayes

The right of John M Hayes to be identified as author of this work has been asserted by the author in accordance with section 77 and 78 of the Copyright, Designs and Patents Act 1988.

ISBN 978-1-83538-555-5 (Paperback)
978-1-83538-556-2 (Hardback)
978-1-83538-557-9 (E-Book)

Book Cover Design and Book Layout by:
Maple Publishers
www.maplepublishers.com

Published by:
Maple Publishers
Fairbourne Drive, Atterbury,
Milton Keynes,
MK10 9RG, UK
www.maplepublishers.com

A CIP catalogue record for this title is available from the British Library.

All rights reserved. No part of this book may be reproduced or translated by any form or by any means, electronic or mechanical, including photocopying, recording or by any information storage and retrieval system without written permission from the author.

The views expressed in this work are solely those of the author and do not reflect the opinions of Publishers, and the Publisher hereby disclaims any responsibility for them. This book should not be used as a substitute for the advice of a competent authority, admitted or authorized to advise on the subjects covered.

CONTENTS

PART ONE

ACKNOWLEDGEMENTS 4

FOREWORD 5

Chapter 1 – Part One 7

Chapter 2 – EARLY INFLUENCES 8

Chapter 3 – HASLAND 14

Chapter 4 – THE DISCOVERY OF ANOTHER WORLD 24

PART TWO
THE FIRST WATERSHED

Chapter 1 – RELIGION TAKES OVER 39

Chapter 2 – A MARRIED MAN AT NINETEEN 46

Chapter 3 – THE COLLEGE YEARS 49

Chapter 4 – ALL SET FOR A UNIVERSITY EDUCATION 66

Chapter 5 – FOLLOWING A VOCATION DONCASTER AND CHESHAM – FOURTEEN YEARS 78

Chapter 6 – ANOTHER WATERSHED – JUNE 1972 A LIBERATING, LIFE-ENHANCING EXPERIENCE 95

Chapter 7 – A WORLD OF UNREALITY OXFORD – MICHAELMAS TERM 1974 ROOM V5 REGENT'S PARK COLLEGE 105

Chapter 8 – A DISASTROUS MARRIAGE TRINITY BAPTIST CHURCH, CHESHAM 111

Chapter 9 – MY LIFE TURNED UPSIDE DOWN 148

Chapter 10 – FROM FAITH TO FAITHLESS 154

Chapter 11 – THE PURPOSE OF LIFE IS TO ENJOY BEING ALIVE 161

ACKNOWLEDGEMENTS

My heartfelt thanks to Stephanie Waterfall, my long-suffering PA who typed and re-typed the script so many times.

To Ian Johnston CB who volunteered to proofread my script but proceeded to assist in the editing of the book. He also kindly composed the foreword and the note on the back cover.

FOREWORD

This is the extraordinary, true story of an awkward, thoughtful boy, born into the restricted world of a pit community, who turned to religion as his escape into the wider world. The poor local schools offered no preparation for the 11+, and tragically, he did not understand what was being offered when subsequently, the teacher in his secondary school, recognising his academic potential, got him an offer of a grammar school place, which he declined.

From Sunday school to youth clubs his talents as a leader and preacher sparkled, and at twenty-one, he left the colliery world to train to be a full-time pastor. Inner doubts about the depth of this belief soon surfaced. He was tormented for two decades by feelings of academic inferiority and being a clerical imposter. Nevertheless he persisted with his studies gaining a degree in Divinity. He married very young to a woman two and a half years older who became a qualified teacher. Throughout his marriage, he doubted his capabilities as a parent and husband.

Once he qualified, despite this religious torment, he was a storming success as an evangelist, significantly increasing his congregations. But disaster struck in his second big church, in the form of a split between traditionalists and modernists. With his marriage under stress, he fell for Maggie, a married member of his congregation. He lost his chapel and finally his beliefs, and after further years of trying, his first marriage.

Still searching for meaning in his life he tried politics and eventually discovered Humanism.

Meanwhile he founded a successful professional business and is now an affluent philanthropist able to enjoy the better things in life, along with Maggie who he tracked down and married many years later.

As a colloquial autobiography, part written from memory and part from diaries, it is a convincing social study of the mores of his mining community, of family life, and of the extraordinary hypocrisy of the church, and of the life of a pastor in the 1960s and 1970s.

His seeking meaning and fellowship, and fulfilment shine through. But most of all it is an astonishingly frank and detailed account of his struggles with his faith and his journey to faithlessness.

A true friend.

Part One

Chapter One
EARLY INFLUENCES

"I don't know where our John came from!" My mother's exclamation was heard throughout childhood; was I really so different? Well, yes! For some reason, I never quite fitted into my parents' culture. Despite Bill and Nellie providing a good and secure upbringing, aspects of the way they lived never appealed to me. Perhaps, it was from about the age of ten this became noticeable even to the wider family.

Dad was part of a large family. All his brothers, like their dad before them, worked down the pit; they were coal miners. When I was growing up in the 1940s, most of them still lived at the family home in the hovel built by the owners of Pilsley Colliery. One major thing that upset my fastidious nature was the outside WC; well, it wasn't even a water closet, rather it was no more than a large piece of wood with a hole in the middle! All the human waste had to be collected, from time to time, by council workers. (Although, at home, our lavatory was also outside, at least the waste could be flushed away!) So, it was at a very early stage that I developed a strong aversion to visiting the Hayes' home in Pilsley.

Perhaps, having been born in the maternal grandparents' home in North Wingfield on 18th February 1940, it was inevitable I was drawn towards them. Although, like dad's family, they were working class and Grandad Knowles also worked down the pit, their home, as well as other aspects of their life, stood in contrast to the Hayes' clan. There were aspects of the Knowles' household that strongly appealed to the impressionable lad that I was. Grandma Sarah was, for instance, fastidiously clean, neat and tidy, as was her home. A fabulous cook and baker—her custard tarts were to die for! (I never forgot them, and they were to become a feature in my life in the middle age.)

Another reason, I gravitated towards the maternal grandparents was that, as a family, mam, dad, Pat, Trevor and I had tea with them most Sundays. What a tea it was! Pork pie; boiled ham; corned-beef; tomatoes; lettuce; celery (in a large glass jug); cucumber and onions chopped up and served in vinegar; and beetroot—followed by an array of cakes, often a large home-made fruit cake. Finally, out came the tinned fruit, perhaps peaches or apricots and evaporated milk—and this was accompanied by grandma's thinly sliced bread and butter, to make sure everyone was well and truly replete. Where did we put it all, just a few hours after the two-course lunch we'd eaten at home! We ate 'dinner' at about 12 o'clock before walking to Hasland Toll Bar to catch the North Wingfield bus.

My contact with grandma and grandad became more intense when, in the junior school years, they invited me to stay with them for part of the summer holidays. It was then that I appreciated 'superficial' things, such as the table being set, formally, for dinner and grandad Ben polishing his black shoes until one could almost see one's face in them. This caring for tidiness and order, somehow, suited me. Having even everyday things being done well was what I liked so much. These feelings of mine were reinforced by also staying with grandad's sister, Aunty Mable, who lived in Sheffield. She and her husband, Jimmy, had married late in life, so they had no children in the house. Perhaps, this is why they gave me a holiday with them several consecutive years. Aunty Mable was, like grandma, houseproud and an excellent cook (Both of them had worked 'in service' and cooked for others. Aunty, especially cooked for the family of one of Sheffield's steel magnates.).

Uncle Jimmy also provided me with some different experiences. Once he took me to a cutlery works to which, as a postman, he delivered post; we were given a tour of the works, accompanied by explanations. Towards the end, we entered the delivery room. On seeing cutlery being packed for delivery to India, and other parts of the Empire, I was dumbstruck. Several times, I was taken to Millhouses Park, and, on one occasion, Uncle Jimmy, just for the fun of it, took me for a tram ride from Crookes to the terminus at Handsworth at the other end of the city. I was also treated to trips to the Speedway and the Greyhound Races. Several coach day trips were taken to North Wales. Once, when the coach paused so we could see the bridge over the Menai Straits, I obtained the driver's permission to run over the bridge so that I could set foot in Anglesey. The driver generously waited for me! Aunty Mable, at least once, took me to Coles restaurant for lunch, and though it may only have been beans on toast, the new experience of eating out was enjoyable. On many an evening, we played cards, especially a game called 'Queeny' where we gambled with pennies and half-pennies. Friday evening was fish night, when I was sent down the street to buy fish and chips. There was a record player in the house, and it was on this equipment that I first heard the song 'I belong to Glasgow;' throughout life, especially for the two years I lived there, I've remembered the words and sung the piece. One New Year's eve, I had been invited to stay, but they had an ulterior motive. Just before midnight, my face was blackened, and I was asked to go outside until, on the stroke of midnight, I was to 'let in' the new year.

Oh, so many experiences for me! Somehow, my home life provided none of this. I was stimulated, and I wanted to experience more, to be living a fuller, more interesting existence.

Life at home didn't lack interest, but mam and dad seemed to be missing out so much, in my opinion. Of course, at the time, my feelings were vague, and I was unable to articulate what was going through my mind. I really did want more, to have a fuller, more interesting life than was afforded by the current working-class culture. No doubt, it's an exaggeration, but my extended Hayes family had little more than football, the 'pictures' and the pub! The cinema certainly caught my interest, but surely, there was much, much more to experience.

This 'difference' in me began to almost alienate me from the family. I was beginning to see that life was not just a party—there was so much more potential. This appealed to my increasingly serious nature. 'Serious' was not an epithet one could apply to dad. It must be said, however, much later in life, I very much came to appreciate the jolly nature of dad's people, something that mother had at first responded to, and then lived out. Why it was that their happy-go-lucky, laughter-loving style didn't appeal to the young John, I'm at a loss to understand. No wonder mam repeated: "I don't know where our John came from." I do know that my outlook was only reinforced, as a few years later, I adopted religion, which eventually, literally, took over my life.

As for the Hayes family, Grandad Hayes left the pit due to ill health. He had the very good fortune to be appointed as steward at Pilsley Miners Welfare, where he was provided with a good modern house. It was then, hypocritically, I would sometimes call so that I was able to have a hot, steamy bath! (At this time, we were still living in the house that was without a bathroom.) Baths were taken in a new house in Pilsley! I very well remember luxuriating in the hot water in my early teens. In those years, it was also fun to visit events such as the village carnival. At least once, dad set me up with a stall outside the Welfare selling pop and crisps. I loved this! Now, I was doing something useful and earning money too! Dad was always ambitious and worked hard to improve his lot, and to some extent, I inherited this attitude from him. At one carnival, I took part in a singing talent competition that led to me joining a concert party.

Sadly, my improved contact with the Hayes family didn't draw me any closer to them. Conversation was quite limited. For example, I don't recollect grandad ever talking to me! Clearly, it was going to be somewhere else that I would find the stimulation my serious nature required.

It was sometime before, it was explained to me that Grandma Knowles had been married before and that uncle Stanley, whose family joined us at grandma's place for Sunday tea, was the son of her first marriage to a Mr Sellars. This man had been a good friend of Grandad Ben. When they both went to war, Ben voluntarily made a promise to look after his friend's wife and child should his friend get killed. This is what happened… Ben, himself, was badly wounded in a leg and spent time in a military hospital. (He died at the age of seventy-four in Chesterfield Royal Hospital whilst being treated for these wounds that had never healed.) I have a feeling that Ben, who worked at the pit, never had a shower there like the other miners because he felt uneasy about his wounds being exposed. He cycled home after each shift and washed down at the kitchen sink. One of my happiest memories is of my waiting in the front garden to look for him coming down the hill; he always gave me one of his lovely smiles.

Apparently, and understandably, Ben was very fond of Nellie, his only child. Sarah seemed unable to show the same warmth, and Nellie always felt that her half-brother Stanley was a favourite. As a very young girl, whilst the family lived in Morton and before moving to North Wingfield, grandad found a small walking stick for his daughter. Then, on Sundays, they went together to a pub in the next village. Ben also took Nellie dancing; his wife being unwilling to accompany him.

When Nellie was older, she was given jobs to do in the house. After leaving school, having had little education, she worked as a waitress in Woodhead's Café in Chesterfield. In all weathers, she cycled several miles six days a week to get to and from work. Her mother then expected her to do work in the house and, of course, Stanley, being the male, did nothing! To myself, grandma was able to show some affection, though never in the form of a hug or kiss. It is quite understandable that Nellie quickly responded to the family who showed their emotions so openly. She said that dad's sisters took her to their hearts, treating her as one of them. She often stayed with them when courting dad, despite necessarily having to share a bed with several. Her mother expressed shock and disapproval that Nellie chose to stay with them when she had 'such a good home.' Grandma had no awareness of how much the love-starved Nellie enjoyed the down-to-earth affection of dad's sisters.

In later life, when dad's sister Mary was asked where everyone slept when they were children, she explained, "the youngest ones slept in mam and dad's room; the others were divided, by sex, into the second room and the landing." On the landing, just imagine, and with no bathroom or indoor toilet! Yet, Nellie preferred this to her own very comfortable home—that reveals so much!

During childhood, Nellie had been sickly. Stanley, her half-brother, told me that she was often plagued by illness. She must have been tough though. (When at the age of almost eighty-eight she lay dying, a nurse said about her, "she has a strong heart.")

Because of the relationship with her mother, she was quite unprepared for many aspects of adulthood. I was told, more than once, about what happened at my birth in the house on Willamthorpe Road, North Wingfield. At one point, when mother was in labour, the midwife scolded grandmother with the words: "You should be ashamed of yourself; this girl doesn't know what's happening." Apparently, my mother was unclear about where I was to come out into the world! In later life, mother shared with me not only the details of birth but also the circumstances of how I was conceived.

One night, Nellie had been out, perhaps, to a dance or cinema. On walking home, dad said to his girlfriend, "Let's just go down this lane." His intentions were revealed when he took out a condom. Instantly, Nellie screamed her reaction, "You can't use that Bill. It may give me TB!" And so, it transpired, rather than get TB, she got JMH—that's me! It was characteristic of mother, in her advanced years, that she happily related this story. Whoever she was with, she would come out with stories or elements that made people laugh; she had become more of a Hayes than a Knowles. In old age, I took her to Paris, New York (on Concorde) and to several excellent hotels in England. She never seemed intimidated. She was now 'comfortable in her own skin.' Whoever we met, however important, she regaled them with stories, mainly of her life—and how she loved making people laugh. Sometimes, it was slightly embarrassing, yet, obviously, she won the respect, even admiration, of people.

Chapter Two
HASLAND

So much then for my family! My earliest memories of home were those of living at 1 Meakin Street, Hasland. Hasland was part of the Borough of Chesterfield. The house had been condemned, but, after the war as well as during it, there was a very serious shortage of housing. Some couples, on becoming married, were obliged to live only in rooms. For a short while, my dad's brother Charlie and his wife Doris actually stayed with us. The house had a very small patch of garden to the front but, to my delight, a long, though narrow, garden at the back. This provided me with entertainment—playing inside the air-raid shelter or building bonfires for November 5th, as well as excavating for a sort of coal mine (as though we didn't have enough coal from my dad's colliery). The only sitting room was tiny, but we ate and lived there. Our kitchen, with its cement floor, sported a large copper in one corner as well as a sink and a gas geyser, which provided hot water. Besides the outside lavatory, there was a large coalhouse.

One of my very earliest memories, which is still vivid, is of the day of 20th May 1942. Mam and I were standing with our back to a roaring coal fire, me in dungarees and mother in a dress, uplifted at the back to get the fire heat on her legs. Following a knock at the door, a woman carrying a bag walked in. Without more ado, she went upstairs with mam. That was the last I saw of mam until she came down with a baby, my sister Pat or Patricia Anne as she was later christened. What a complete surprise! Of course, not only had no warning been given to me but also never a word was uttered about where Pat had come from. Is there any wonder that in those days youngsters spoke of babies being delivered by storks! The whole business of procreation was never spoken of. Both mam and dad were far too shy to raise the subject. Not until 1959, on the eve of my getting married, did dad refer to the subject. But, then on the day before the wedding, he drove me into Worksop and encouraged me to buy condoms from the chemist. Even then, nothing else reveals how little he told me about the subject, except the fact that I only bought two condoms for the whole honeymoon!

Margaret, in the event, became pregnant at that time, although she miscarried soon afterwards.

The twelve or so years in Hasland were quite happy ones. From the age of four, I attended the Eyre Street Primary School, starting in the nursery where we were put into bed for a nap every afternoon. Transferring from this cosy environment to my first classroom caused some trepidation. The very first day, sitting near the back of the class, I began to cry. When the kindly Miss Tubbs saw me and then asked, "John, are you crying?" The reply came, "No Miss, I've just got water in my eyes!" From that moment, I settled down well enough.

Even at a tender age, I made my own way to and from school, despite having to cross the main road. To illustrate the potential danger of this, one only has to relate an anecdote. One morning, Jack Hall, a boy in my class, caught up with me as we reached the main road at Hasland Toll Bar. A double-decker bus was stationary; I decided to wait until it moved away—not Jack! He ran across the road behind the bus and was hit by a car—the driver had no chance. The picture of a flood of blood running down Jack's neck remains vivid to this day. Fortunately, Jack quickly recovered and was soon back at school. It was sometime later, having been called out of class and into the hallway, Miss Lockwood asked me what I'd witnessed. Seeing a letter in her hand, or at least the envelope marked 'On His Majesty's Service,' I felt somewhat uneasy that King George should want anything to do with me! My account must have exonerated the poor car driver.

One very enjoyable feature of the school was the nature table. I do think it was Miss Haynes' nature talks that awoke in me a love of nature—an experience that has been profoundly important throughout my whole life. Miss Haynes encouraged her pupils to bring objects for the nature table—conkers, pussy willow, acorns, catkins and even live creatures like tadpoles in jam jars. I loved it. She was a Londoner and frequently referred to Kew Gardens. I reckon these classroom lessons were formative in my education. Bless you, Miss Haynes! Certainly, I enjoyed nature. In the light evenings of late spring, a song thrush could be heard outside my bedroom window; the singing was ecstatic—surely, everyone thrills to the sound of this wonderful bird.

Two vivid memories from this time were, firstly, the street party on Victory in Europe Day and, shortly afterwards, the garage party on VJ day. For the first celebration, the whole street was decorated; trimmings were hung across the street from house to house. Everyone sat down by trestle tables, which lined the street. At five years old, little detail was remembered but for the obvious happy atmosphere. The second event, more low-key, was just for the children. Somehow, we all managed to squash into the pub garage at the end of the street.

Other highlights, a few years on, were holidays at Skegness Holiday Camp. Shortly after the end of the war in 1947, the camp was opened opposite the already existing Miners Convalescent Home. Miners from the Derbyshire pits were offered a week's subsidised holiday. From the very beginning, it proved to be exciting. A special train would pull into Chesterfield Central (one of three stations in those days). I revelled in the train ride. For several years, it was our annual week's holiday. There were activities for the children, such as competitive sports. At night, I slept with lots of others in a comfortable dormitory. The lovely nurse, who was with us all night, made for a very cosy, safe environment. In the later years, I took part in talent competitions. One year, the house was brought down as I sang 'Jerusalem,' and with it won first prize (more on singing later).

Another happy memory of my early years is assisting mam with Christmas baking. She made loads of jam tarts, mince pies, coconut tarts and lemon tarts. My job was to cut out the tops and place them over the fillings. The finished products were placed on large plates and taken into the huge pantry, more like a cellar, under the stairs.

Another significant memory comes from one Christmas Eve. There was no Christmas tree—surprisingly, as we almost always had one. But, on this Christmas Eve, after dark, dad asked me to put on a coat to go out with him. After walking to the top of Calow Lane, the main road was crossed. Before us, was the high wall around Hasland Hall, once a private estate, now a secondary school. The wall was scaled, the top of a holly tree felled and there we had it, that year's Christmas tree! Feelings of uncertainty and anxiety filled my mind as the holly was carried down the lane. Those feelings have not been forgotten to this day. Dad was fundamentally a good man, but, on the other hand, he was regarded as 'a bit of a lad.' Kind-hearted, generous as any Hayes, yet he sometimes crossed over the line, though never in a serious criminal way.

Back to childhood days in Hasland. Not being gregarious, there was nevertheless some group engagement. Meakin Street was dimly lit by a few gas lamps. Conditions were ideal for playing games like hide and seek. There were a few children living on our street, and on winter evenings, we would join up to play. The street itself wasn't adequate for hide and seek so we commandeered the gardens. At times, I was afraid of getting hurt—there seemed to be quite a lot of glass around, apart from anything else.

These play times were about the only opportunity I took for socialising—fundamentally, my own company was preferred. It seems I didn't feel an affinity with anyone. No school friends were ever made in fifteen years of education, and the only lad on Meakin Street whom I regarded as a friend was a Roy Burbage. He had two older brothers and was obviously spoilt. His father was charged with sexual assault of boys. He tried it on me in our house one day even whilst Roy was present. Fortunately, the assault was mild—he put a hand down the back of my trousers and stroked my bottom. Although it was discomfiting, nothing was ever said about it. Not long after the incident, and before his criminal trial, poor Mr Burbage strolled onto the moors to commit suicide.

The only other time anything like this happened to me was when a girl neighbour was babysitting me, and she touched the parts of my body she shouldn't have. This must have been when I was still very young, certainly before puberty.

There is no doubt a great deal of this activity existed. In my later professional life, through providing a counselling service, my eyes were opened as to the prevalence of this and, indeed, far worse sexual abuses in the community.

It may have been shyness, yet I suspect it was more to do with my nature that my activities in childhood were generally solo. Anyhow, I developed an inner life that didn't require relationships. Perhaps, it is significant that an almost friendless John invented an imaginary friend. This must have been when I was about ten or eleven, but the 'friendship' lasted for at least two years. How it worked was that, on going to bed, my 'friend' would come to talk and take instructions. 'To take instructions?' Yes, because I was a 'Boss,' and he worked for me. Sometimes in the autumn, I would start thinking about building a site for Christmas and earlier for November 5th, bonfire night. The arrangements were for the enjoyment of 'the people,' presumably my people! It occurs to me that this experience may have been an indication that later in life I would enjoy organising things, as well as a foretaste of the experience of leadership in one form or another that transpired. Many people in childhood have an imaginary friend, but it is surely significant that my 'friend' addressed me as 'Boss.'

Another of my 'solo' activities was building an annual November 5th bonfire. I revelled in collecting bonfire material from the fields off Calow Lane. Not only did I collect dead wood, but also taking with me a hatchet, I broke off branches to make up a huge bonfire. (A streak of dad's naughtiness obviously was passed onto me!)

August 10th 1948 saw another member joining our household. He had been born in hospital, unlike mother's first two babies. The first time I saw him was when he was being pushed up the street in a pram after being collected from hospital.

Neither Pat nor Trevor were labelled with 'being different' as I was. Significantly, as they grew up, each of them loved the Hayes' family but didn't at all take to Grandma Knowles. Perhaps, this had something to do with the fact that I was the only one of the three ever invited to stay at Grandma Knowles in the school holidays. Pat was always relaxed with the jolly Hayes' tribe; she was always very much one of them. Trevor also appreciated their attitude to life but, as an adult, found other values that were important to him. Whilst always believing in the importance of ensuring one had 'a good time,' he became convinced of the importance of hard work and endeavoured to improve one's lot (of course, that was like dad). Starting off as an employed joiner, he graduated from managing projects, like building a hospital in Algeria to establishing his own building business. For many years, he specialised in pre-concrete structures but branched out into barn conversions and building new houses. But what really took Trevor away from the Hayes' values, was politics; he did the unthinkable and became a Tory! In this respect then, Trevor broke with family tradition—he was the one who was 'different.' Despite having a brother and sister, I remained quite isolated. During the whole time at home, I never developed a relationship with Pat, so much so, there was an absence of conversation between us. Contact or engagement with Trevor wasn't much better, but this greatly improved much later in life.

With the arrival of Trevor, there were five people in a two-bedroomed house; we were overcrowded. Yet, it was about four years before we were re-housed just down the road to 53 Heathcote Drive, an National Coal Board (NCB) new estate, built for coal miners. (More of that later, I'm getting ahead of myself.)

At the age of seven, I was transferred to Hasland Junior School. As on my first day at Eyre Street, I felt unhappy. Standing in the playground of the junior school on my first day, with my back to the wall and feeling lost and lonely, I again found myself crying. But I needn't have worried; it turned out that my subsequent four years at the school were quite enjoyable. It was here that I began to enjoy singing. Mr Greaves, our headmaster, led music classes—my soprano voice was just right for it. One particular melody, with its melancholy words, moved me—and it still does. "Oh, Shenandoah I long to see thee." Once a year, all the area junior school choirs assembled in Bradbury Hall for an afternoon concert. There was always a professional conductor in charge. To me, these were wonderful times, singing in a massed choir.

I must elaborate on how grandparents and aunty and uncle left their mark on my life. It is not that my grandma or my aunty were of a different class but, interestingly, both had associated with another culture; Aunty Mable cooked for the Fearnehoughs and steel magnets, and grandma cooked for the Masons at their Chesterfield Lodge. Their cuisine and dining standards were more middle class, and I took it all on board. There is no doubt that I respected their standards and began to aspire. This made me different! The downside is that I became judgemental and critical of mam and dad. Their life seemed somewhat restricted, rather boring.

At school, I remained shy and isolated. My fastidiousness also, one day, caused shame when, due to a reluctance to use school toilets, I filled my pants (This was at the age of ten.). Amazingly, the accident remained undetected, and it wasn't until I reached home that a clean-up took place!

Disappointingly, despite always being in the top class (that is top of three), my education was impaired through lack of motivation; English, especially spelling, was always troublesome. Therefore, I failed the dreaded Eleven Plus, which was the only passport to a grammar school. Without any guidance, parents were left to make important decisions. On discussing it with mam and especially dad, we chose William Rhodes, with Peter Webster as second choice. The latter was my destiny, a supposedly good boys' school for technical education; in reality, it was a thoroughly poor school (more of that later).

One of the highlight incidents at Hasland Green Juniors was an encounter with a bully. This lad had a reputation, and he must have thought I was a soft target. It was, no doubt, obvious that I wasn't robust or sporty but rather sensitive and nervous. It became apparent that he was out to get me! This all came about without provocation. Fortunately, I could run, and, on several days, coming out of school, it was easy to escape him. One day, however, he was able to block me, and a fight ensued. People gathered, and some shouted encouragement to me. Then, all of a sudden, the violence subsided; I had given him a bloody nose, and he sheepishly crept away. Never again did he trouble me.

In September 1951, I started at the Peter Webster Secondary School on Whittington Moor. Reaching the school involved travel on two buses, one from Hasland to Chesterfield and another from there to Whittington Moor. Looking back, this must have encouraged my isolation and sense of being different. As I was living so far from the area where most fellow pupils lived, one never met up after school. The catchment area of the school was a poor area, and the dominant interest amongst the staff, as well as pupils, was football. I came to hate the school, again increasing my sense of isolation.

Outside school, life became more interesting. Opportunities arose to perform on stage, by singing. Not long after starting secondary school, an opportunity was afforded to me to sing solo in an amateur concert party. My dad was always looking out for opportunities for my advancement, as he was for his own. It was at one of the carnival days at Pilsley Miners Welfare that he pushed me on stage in a talent competition. Afterwards, an Eddie Burnham, a working-class man living in a council house, invited me to join his concert party. He lived in Stonebroom, which meant my having to travel several miles by bus to his house for so-called rehearsals; it was all very amateurish, but the travelling and performing were enjoyable, which continued until my voice broke. Usually, performances took place in chapels (There was an abundance of them in those days—predominantly, Methodist.). Once, however, a performance was laid on at what was then called Mickleover Lunatic Asylum. In the huge hall, it seemed that hundreds of drab-looking individuals, mainly male, made up the audience, with wardens, of course, looking on. Well, do I remember a disturbing image that has stayed with me throughout life? On alighting from the coach, I spotted, quite high up the building, a person apparently cleaning a window on the inside. Following the concert and the tea that had been provided, I looked up to see the person at the same window, still cleaning it.

The Eddie Burnham concerts built up my confidence and were a source of pleasure. Ironically, although I loved to sing, my singing teacher grew exasperated with me because I never practised to improve performance. The repertoire was extremely limited because I couldn't, or wouldn't, bother to learn the words. So, one sang 'Down in the Glen,' 'At the End of the Day,' and, my all-time favourite that won me plaudits, 'Jerusalem.'

My performances were for charity and personal pleasure, but, on rare occasions, as at Skegness, I did receive a financial reward. A quite bizarre event was when dad arranged for me to sing one night at the Holmewood Club. Not being of age for sitting in the pub, I was taken in by the landlady to wait inside her house until the time arrived for me to go on stage. This assignment earned me some money.

Singing lessons only lasted a short time—boy sopranos have a short shelf life. I'm sure, however, the lessons that were provided by a woman from the chapel did have, at least, a marginal impact on my performance.

Once my voice settled down, after 'breaking,' I enthusiastically joined the chapel choir as a tenor. It gave me a feeling of pride to stand singing beside Mr Slatcher. The choir met in the week for practice. Of course, it wasn't the hymns that required us to do this but the anthems. Singing anthems was another new experience, one which wasn't always very enjoyable, but I could sing my head off forever, when it came to 'Handel's Messiah.' Quite often, a Sunday evening service was rounded off with what became one of my favourite hymns, 'The Day Thou Gavest Lord is Ended.' Wow, when we got to the last verse, the feeling of power was tremendous!

"The sun that bade us wake is waking our brethren neath the western sky;" and "hour by hour fresh lips are making Thy wonderous doings heard on high." The words gave one a deep sense of belonging to a God-loving and universal community; it was so inspiring, and the tune itself so matched the words and reinforced the emotion.

Singing provided such joy. No doubt, it was one of the things that drew me towards chapel services. It is of significance that walking proudly, with shoulders back, on Hasland Toll Bar to the Methodist Church on Sunday mornings, it wasn't a Bible being carried but a Methodist Hymn Book; oh, how the Wesley hymns lifted my spirits! Even now, as an atheist, I can, and do, heartily sing hymns such as 'And can it be that I should gain an interest in the Saviour's blood' (This hymn is often alluded to as being the Methodists' anthem.).

Later in life, on becoming deeply religious, it was theology contained in the text of these hymns that I appreciated as much as the tunes. The most meaningful carol to my mind was 'Hark the Herald Angels Sing,' full of fine, evangelical theology.

Chapter Three
THE DISCOVERY OF ANOTHER WORLD

"I don't know where our John came from." In the eyes of our extended family, not just those of mother, I didn't seem to quite belong. Well before teenage years, there was a discernible seriousness in me that wasn't characteristic of any other family member. Aunty Hylma, who was only a year or two older than me, saw through it all—to her it was snobbishness! Yes, there was an element of this, but there was also something deeper.

Where had this come from? How had it arisen? Perhaps, it had a lot to do with genes. Certainly, long ago, my view was formed that we are, and always will be, not much more than the basic stuff that we're born with. Yet, surely, that is only a major part of it. Is it nature or nurture?

There can be no doubt that in my case another factor had a profoundly moulding influence.

From a very early age, I came under the influence of Hasland Methodist Church—first of all, through Sunday school. For me, it was a lovely experience to sit on a small chair listening to Bible stories and singing songs.

- "Hear the pennies dropping,
- Listen how they fall;
- Everyone for Jesus,
- He shall have them all."

My home background contained nothing like it, but I enjoyed being drawn into this unknown world. The Sunday school was huge.

A massive two-storey building teemed with life on Sunday afternoons. Gradually, other activities became available. For a time, I was a Sunday school teacher. Then, mid-week there was the inters-club, a very junior youth club. The opportunity also arose of attendance at morning service.

What I was hearing in church provoked me into thinking about God. At home, still in Meakin Street, I often looked out of the bedroom window, dazzled by the mass of stars, wondering where it had all come from. These ponderings coincided with RE classes at school when I was about twelve. Mr Hunt, one of the half-decent teachers, gave a lecture one day on 'Creation.' This, together with my own bedroom musings, convinced me that there was a God (Naturally, as I'd heard nothing of any other Gods, I conceived of this God as the one who was talked about, and worshipped in the Methodist Church.).

Up to this point, I hadn't gone head over heels with religion. I enjoyed many more things outside religion: films at the cinema; dances on Monday evenings in Hasland Village Hall; and, perhaps, to a greater extent than my peer group—girls!

At church, there was also graduation to the youth club where one was introduced to table tennis, billiards and even drama. The most bizarre activity of all, being an all-male harmonica band. Something that was also surprising was a formal annual dinner. Mr and Mrs Slatcher were the youth leaders—a dedicated couple who profoundly influenced my personal development.

As the connection with the church, or chapel as it was often spoken of, became more intense, especially around the age of thirteen/fourteen, mam expressed a concern that I was taking it all too seriously; "I don't know where our John came from." It isn't surprising that this concern had arisen. Both mam and dad were somewhat baffled at how I was 'turning out.' I had developed a stance of treating life seriously. It was, probably, a year or so after this time when we were living in the Coal Board new house, 53 Heathcote Drive, that a very telling encounter took place with dad. For once, he and I were having a serious conversation, when suddenly dad blurted out the words "I'm afraid to think!" I've never forgotten those words; they are tremendously significant. No other phrase could define the difference there is between me and dad. Even in those early years, I wasn't interested in a 'thoughtless life.' A saying that I only came across much later in life, accurately illustrates my state of mind at the time, although, of course, I couldn't have articulated then.

"It is better to be a dissatisfied Socrates than to be a satisfied pig."

Clearly, even as a youngster, I had acquired a deeply serious approach to life. Sadly, one can say, looking back, this came with a judgemental attitude. (Yes, Aunty Hylma had detected the early stage of this! My brother Trevor insists that he once heard me say to dad, "You're a sinner!") Oh dear, how very judgemental! No doubt to see everything in terms of black or white. But, unfortunately, in my case, it resulted in a measure of alienation from the family. I honestly felt closer to and identified more with the church 'family' than with my natural one.

An example of how my intense engagement with the chapel was, is what happened on Sunday evenings. It must have been from about the age of twelve.

I've already mentioned that, as a family, we spent Sunday afternoons with Grandad and Grandma Knowles.

About 5 p.m., we would sit down for high tea—an enormous feast. The challenge for me was how to enjoy the meal, yet still get back to Hasland in time for the chapel evening service at 6 p.m. Did I manage to do justice to it all? I can't remember! What I do remember was amazing everyone by insisting to rise quickly so that I arrived in Hasland for the 6 p.m. chapel service. (Did I get indigestion? I can't remember.) I would run up to the main road to catch the bus that stopped in Hasland almost outside the chapel door. Incredibly, I don't ever remember being later than arriving as the congregation were singing the first hymn. Well, mam and dad could not be in doubt where my priorities lay. "I don't know where our John came from." This religious zeal was puzzling as not one of my extended family had anything to do with a church.

On a more positive note, yet still reflecting the difference with my parents, involvement with the Methodists, indirectly, awoke and fed a love of nature. One moment in time is quite unforgettable. Mr and Mrs Slatcher took a group of us for a day and night to a centre in Castleton, in the Peak District. On awakening in the morning, before the others, I peeped through the curtains; the view outside sent a thrill all through me. The dramatic countryside was nothing like anything I'd ever seen. From that moment, I've been drawn to the outdoors. Being with and in nature became such an important part of my life experience. (It is difficult to understand why mam and dad never took us into the Peak District, despite it being so accessible.) The sense of wonder at the natural world doesn't seem to have run in the family, yet for me it became a huge and even vital part of living—to exaggerate, it would be difficult.

Mr Slatcher, in particular, also helped my development in another way. To my amazement, he spotted some leadership potential. (I say amazement because other people in the peer group were more clever and, apparently, more confident; I was quite shy.) On Sunday evenings, in the Slatchers' house, after church, I often felt left out when the grammar school contingent discussed physics, chemistry, for example, subjects completely out of my reach. School, for me, was a disaster. Very soon after my arrival at Peter Webster's school, it became quite obvious that the school's claims were a sham. With the exception of a few, the faculty consisted of poor teachers. Pupils were provided with a meagre education. My most shocking personal experience of this occurred in the first week of my second year. It was a science lesson. Each pupil was handed a small new notebook. The master then spoke: "Boys Dictation. The Rules of the Laboratory." The rules of the laboratory—this was as far as our 'top' class had got, despite having spent a whole year in science classes with this teacher! Even at the age of twelve, I had developed a questioning attitude, so on hearing the teacher's words, I blurted out: "This isn't science." "What did you say Hayes?" As I'd hoped, my 'loud whisper' had been heard—it had reached the intended target. Another example of how inadequate the school was, also occurred in the second year. A geography lesson was interrupted by the Deputy Head Mr Hunt. Together with another boy, I was called out, not to be taken outside, but to stand in a corner of the room whilst the lesson proceeded! Tall Mr Hunt looked down on the two of us, "Boys it has been decided that you could be transferred to the grammar school." There had been nothing leading up to this statement, although we knew that the two of us were probably the brightest students in our year. Each of us, in turn, replied to Mr Hunt's query as to whether we might be interested, with the same two words, "No Sir." "No Sir." Unbelievably, that was the last one heard of it. How differently life would have turned out, but there have never been any regrets.

If there was any advantage in being at Peter Webster's school, it was, perhaps, that it provided me with some sex education. Not, of course, that in those days it could have come from formal lessons. No, it was not a teacher but a fellow pupil who was responsible for providing some enlightenment. At twelve years of age, I still had no idea where babies came from.

It was in an art class that some boys sitting behind me were talking about Princess Elizabeth having a baby; they were giggling about the sexual activity she had been involved in. I turned round to say, "Don't be stupid, she wouldn't do that sort of thing!" Frank, one of the boys, who had older sisters and so professed to know about such things, exclaimed, "John do you really not know?" He then referred me to a book in one of the school bookcases that would put me right. From that day, he also took an interest in me, like an elder brother. What motivated him is beyond my ken; I only know that, on another day, he took me into the cloakroom, where there was a mirror, to restyle my hair. From that moment, I sported a nice wave above the forehead. About the same time, I was shown how to tie a Windsor knot.

Continuing my sex education, he instigated a rather unsavoury incident that certainly developed my sex education. Together with two other boys, he dragged me into one of the school toilets to initiate me into the possibilities of puberty. The result was my first experience of having an erection and ejaculation: not the most satisfactory initiation! Sadly, the experience left me with a feeling of being dirty. It also caused me, for years, to be somewhat furtive about sexual activity. A few years later, on becoming increasingly religious, I discovered the Methodist's repressive attitudes. Masturbation caused me a struggle with guilt. It is significant that one of the few books bought at this time was a hard back, published by the Methodist Church entitled, *The Mastery of Sex*. However, I wish I could have discovered the experience of a book published many years later: *The Joy of Sex*, goodness me. I knew it was pleasurable, but the pleasure was corrupted by feelings of guilt. Certainly, for years, the whole attitude to any sexual activity, in practice or just in theory, was grossly distorted. Sex must be mastered, as if it were a bad thing!

This provides the cue to write about my relationship with girls.

Up to the age of sixteen, it was very much coloured by Hollywood films. This was before the roaring sixties, the decade of the so called 'sexual liberation.' So, I was a thorough-going romantic.

The first attraction that comes to mind, happened even before puberty, as an eleven-year-old! At the junior school, a girl called Carol Burgess caught my eye. I looked on, infatuated, when she was playing at horse riding in the park. It must be significant that this memory persists, despite my never having even spoken to her! Any relationship was entirely in the imagination.

Certainly, there was a tendency to seek out potential romantic relationships in the very early teenage years. On my thirteenth birthday, I vividly remember awaking, thinking to myself: I'm now thirteen; in three years' time, I could get married!

Several tentative relationships transpired before my first real long-term girlfriend came along.

One such happened, again when only thirteen, at Skegness Holiday Camp. (I was taught a cautionary lesson!) An older girl had caught my attention. The memory is vague, but I can imagine we went as far as to kiss. (Romantically only, of course!) This contact motivated me to buy the girl a piece of jewellery. On the train journey home, she came along the corridor to find me, reporting that the jewellery had broken. Having offered to have it repaired, she agreed to meet me in town once the repair was done. I excitedly met her expecting to spend some time with her again. Some hope! She accepted the restored gift, then immediately disappeared from my life!

Another similarly brief encounter took place on holiday. This time at Mundersley-on-Sea, Norfolk. Mr and Mrs Slatcher from the chapel had taken a group of us to a Methodist holiday centre for a whole week's holiday. Somehow, on encountering a girl from Withernsea on the Lincolnshire coast, I persuaded her to join me on the beach. Within no time at all, we were lying together below a cliff enjoying some kissing—so much were we carried away, we ended up being late going to dinner. On sheepishly trying to find our table, we were noticed; almost instantly, everyone started clapping—very embarrassing!

(Just deviating from the topic of girls for a moment, I would mention that, on this holiday, Mr Slatcher encouraged me to adopt another leadership opportunity. Some of our group slept in the main house, but a few of us were billeted in a garden hut. I was put in charge! During the night, Norfolk experienced one of its notorious thunderstorms. Mr Slatcher came out, in the middle of the night, to check all was well. To me, to be put in charge, felt like a compliment, and surely it was, to be so trusted with some responsibility.)

Now back to the girls! Some of my contact with the opposite sex was no more than having a dance with a girl, and then walking her home. In fact, I was fourteen going on fifteen, before a steady girlfriend came along.

This time, it became a serious relationship; my first and only long-term girlfriend before I met Margaret, my future wife.

Janice Butcher belonged to one of the Methodist chapel groups who met on Sunday evenings. We rarely met on our own, apart from very occasionally going to the 'pictures.' Like myself, Janice had failed the eleven plus, so she attended Hasland Hall Secondary School. This was a co-ed school unlike Peter Webster. Our relationship lasted about two years. The content was emotional and romantic, rather than overtly sexual. (We didn't need to be reminded that the Methodist view was 'no sex before marriage.') Janice was an only child. She lived with her mother and maternal grandmother in quite a nice house. I frequently walked her home. Her father had been killed by a train as he was working on the line as a platelayer.

Janice didn't do dancing, so we never met for that activity. At least once, I well recollect we cycled to her aunt's house in Darley Dale. The very steep, winding hill off the moor provided a hair-raising experience. (In later life, when travelling either up or down this hill, I've naturally remembered my first real girlfriend.)

Another memory is of going out with a small group, walking near and along the edge of Burbage Moor. We sat on a small bridge, over Burbridge Brook. Someone took a photograph, which I retained for many years. (Sometimes, when Maggie and I are walking in that area, she gets a little prickly—probably, she resents that I ever told her about the day I sat there with Janice. Part of Maggie's problem is that the site is only a few hundred yards from Higger Tor, where I proposed marriage to her!)

There is no doubt the relationship with Janice was very significant. This being so, you may ask "what went wrong?"

Relating what went wrong will once again reveal my naivety, even at the age of sixteen! We had been to the 'pictures,' and as was customary, I walked my girlfriend home afterwards. At the garden gate, before kissing her goodnight, we began to discuss an incident that had taken place whilst we had been watching the film. For once, I had gone beyond kissing; my hand slipped inside her blouse, and I stroked her breast, for quite some time. She didn't protest, so one assumed that she was enjoying the new experience as much as I was.

Our talking about this encounter led to, what for me was, a typically serious conversation about sex. On previous occasions, Janice had told me about the tentative sexual exploits that some girls at her school had got into. She did it though in a sort of code language, as even she was unable to be explicit. Well, on this, what was to be our last night by the garden gate, I expressed a view on sex, which must have shocked her; I was of the view that one only had sexual intercourse to have a baby! At the time, I was bewildered, but later, as I matured, this must have been why she peremptorily jilted me. Who could blame her—what an odd person I must have seemed to her. It was probably the very next day that I knocked on Janice's house door in great distress. Grandma came to the door; at first, she wouldn't let me in, but seeing my tears, she kindly invited me to step inside. I never saw Janice, however.

In the long run, Janice, by her rejection of me, probably saved me from making a mess of my life. It wasn't long after the break-up that I learned that my old rival, Clive, who was a year or two older than me, had got Janice pregnant. Some of the older Methodists were quite judgemental, apparently. Anyway, the couple were promptly married. It was sixteen years later that I met them again—this time proudly standing there, now with three children. (More on this later)

Now, going back to school. It did provide some positive experiences. I wasn't interested in team sports, but I could run. As a sprinter, running the 100 yards or the 220, I was the champion. It was on account of this that the school appointed me captain of the Athletics Team, which participated in the Annual Inter-School Sports Day in Queen's Park, Chesterfield. I was just about the only person from our school to win a race! Pupils at Peter Webster were only interested in, or should I say obsessed by, football. But being appointed captain, was another indication that I may have leadership potential. Unsurprisingly, I was appointed a prefect; although whatever responsibilities that were involved, now escape me.

The primary way in which leadership skills were revealed was through my starting and running a railway club. In the 1950s, most boys, even those at grammar school, were 'train spotters'—they just loved steam trains. Often, railway platforms were crowded with boys spending the day watching trains. Books of information about the various classes of trains, with their individual numbers, and some with names, were produced by one Ian Allan (He must have grown rich on the thousands of books sold.). There were also railway magazines that one could obtain, though I didn't bother with those.

An interest in steam trains was aroused in me whilst still at junior school. At the age of eleven, a Michael Siddall arranged for a small number of us to go 'trainspotting' to Retford. Retford station was on the main London North Eastern Region route between London and Scotland. (Chesterfield was on the Midland route.) Although nationalised in the 1940s, the rolling stock of the previous four main railway companies continued to run on the original company lines— so one saw different locomotives in Retford than in Chesterfield. But, up to this trip to Retford, I had shown no interest at all in railways. This one-day trip dramatically changed that! From the day of this group trip, I often travelled over to Retford, on my own, and the whole day until late in the evening was spent there. During the later secondary school holidays, I would also, on many days, be out of bed early and be sitting on a railway bridge rafter before 8 o'clock. This site was very close to Hasland Shed, one of the hundreds of locomotives depots throughout the country. It was classified as 18c, a figure found at the front of all the locomotives allocated to the shed. Amazingly, considering potential dangers, I was sometimes allowed to wonder around. These depots were called 'Roundhouses' because they were circular and in the centre was a turntable; engines were parked at angles facing this turntable. (Of the hundreds of such places, only one working site has survived, and it is at Barrowhill, just a few miles from the centre of Chesterfield. The building was saved and is now used by a group of enthusiasts.)

This interest in trains was an obsession with me. At school, I began to organise trips for a small group of boys. We visited Tamworth, for instance, where we could 'spot' locomotives on the main west route from London to Scotland. Passes were sometimes obtained so we could visit engine sheds or, even, railway workshops where locomotives were built. These places included Crew, Doncaster and Derby. My responsibilities included arranging travel, by train of course! Once, I came unstuck! A coach had been booked for a daytrip to Tamworth, but as the day approached, hardly any boys wanted to go. As a result, none of us went. Just a few weeks afterwards, I was called out of class; someone wanted to speak to me. This person was a railway employee. He gave me a ticking off. "A whole reserved coach travelled empty from Chesterfield to Tamworth." Oh dear! Fortunately, despite this, I wasn't banned from making future reservations. Surprisingly, when school prizes were announced, I was awarded one for my railway club. Well, it probably was an acknowledgement of the initiative, and the leadership I'd shown. The funny thing is that for the book prize I chose *The Observers Book of Birds*. This was another interest that arose during these years. (The prize was presented, as all were, at speech day, which was held in the local civic theatre.)

An incident that reveals my obsession with trains was something that occurred in the summer of 1953. All the train spotters in the town were boys, apart from a stunningly attractive grammar school girl. She was also an athlete. In the same year that I became inter-schools champion in the 220 yards, she also triumphed in her event, representing the girls' grammar school. Like other successful athletes, we were invited to join in a day trip to the 3 A's championships at the White City, London. The day arrived, and I found myself sitting in the stadium bored out of my mind. Suddenly, there was a tap on my shoulder—it was this girl. "Shall we go to Paddington, John?" I didn't wait to be asked twice. Most of the day was spent on Paddington station. There we saw locomotives of the Great Western Region, something one could never expect to encounter in Chesterfield. And so, what would have been, for both of us, a boring experience, turned out to be, instead, something very exciting! Apart from anything else, this story illustrates that though I could sprint, I had no more interest in athletics than in any other sport!

What now seems remarkable is that leadership roles were adopted, despite my being so shy. Perhaps, it was nothing more than a huge enthusiasm for a topic that pushed out the feelings of uncertainty and inferiority. In any case, these underlying factors persisted well into adult life. There can be no doubt, however, that the several opportunities to show leadership, both at school and at church, provided a foundation for roles played in later years. It is a fact that whatever interests I pursued, as an adult, always resulted in me being appointed or recognised for leadership roles—be it religion, politics, or walking, for example.

From the age of thirteen, I had a job. The first one was as a paper boy; mine was a morning round, seven days a week. One Christmas, dad and mam bought me a bike, and it was on this that the round was done. There was no basket on the front, unlike the bikes of a rival newsagent, who provided sit-up bikes for his boys. For me, it was a case of carrying a large bag over the shoulder, which affected my balance, but I wanted the money—ten shillings for the week's work. Of course, the job entailed an early start, although not so early on Sundays. It was a relief when, at last, the other newsagent employed me. He provided a proper, purpose-made bike and paid the handsome sum of fifteen shillings—a 50% improvement for me—and a shorter round!

From about the age of fourteen, I also found a Saturday job working for Hunters, the grocer. This also involved cycling, delivering groceries. It did not ride well, despite a purpose-built bike being provided. One Saturday morning, I was engaged delivering to a customer in the next village of Grassmore. The load was heavy and wasn't easy to balance. On turning off the main road into the customer's road, I fell over. Some breakages occurred, but the customer was altogether sympathetic; however, this was the last time I was expected to accept the assignment.

When it came to leaving school, at fifteen, it was the manager at Hunters who persuaded me that there were good prospects in the grocery trade. Because my birthday was in the month of February, I finished my education at Easter after only two terms in the final year. (A somewhat pathetic arrangement I thought, even at the time.)

This first job was not a success! The hours were nine until six. Frequently, I found myself alone in the afternoons, which were, generally, quiet. How the time would drag! Quite often, a few minutes before six, a customer would enter—sometimes followed by another. It was unusual to lock up shop and be away by 6 p.m. One or two things stand out in my memory. The manager of the shop was an unpleasant sort; he had a beautiful and gentle wife whom I suspected was abused. She sometimes popped into the shop and always spoke kindly to me. One thing about my boss really upset me, though I didn't have the confidence to speak about it, was the way he took advantage of one of his customers. This woman had a large family who bought all her groceries from Hunters. Sometimes, she asked for credit. This was strictly not allowed, but the manager did allow it, and then unbeknown to the lady, added something to her bill every week; presumably, she never checked the items, but I witnessed this deceit on a weekly basis.

There were times, when it was very quiet, I was given two special jobs to do. Eggs, for some reason, were not sold in packs, as now; a lot of them were kept in a large basket—it's a wonder more were not broken. My task was to fill a bucket with water, then, one by one, put the eggs in the water; the ones that floated were kept, and the others that sank were thrown away—they were obviously bad.

It was the second task that I found most distasteful. There being no refrigeration, sides of bacon were hung in a cool pantry. Have you guessed it? My job was to scrape off any maggots!

It didn't take long for me to think about an alternative career. At school, having been good in maths and machine drawing, I had aspired to be an engineering draughtsman. Now, surveying came into my mind. Before long, I found myself at the NCB's Regional Training Centre. There was no way for me to jump into an apprenticeship for surveying, however. Once I'd been allocated to Williamthorpe Colliery, where dad worked, I was given a day-release at Chesterfield College—and paid handsomely for it! The condition was that I also attended two evenings for further study. My intention was to pass some exams that could help me find an opening into surveying. Before this could even possibly happen, I decided to forget a career 'down-under' and opted instead to become a clerk in the timekeeper's office. Much cleaner and far less dangerous! Just a few months before this, however, I was working underground, doing cleaning up jobs or working a conveyor belt. Well, do I remember working all alone beside a conveyor belt shovelling up coal that had fallen off the conveyor? Once a patch of ground had been cleared, I would open a bag, like a bag of cement, and, by hand, throw the 'snow dust' all around. The object of this exercise was to lessen the danger of an explosion. Eventually, having been told I would be expected to do shift work, I explained to dad I didn't want to. Somehow, dad was brilliant at making connections, and before I knew it, he had persuaded Mr Rimmer, the undermanager of his seam, to set me on as his errand boy. Goodness me, what a 'non-job' this turned out to be. Each morning, I was expected to call at the Overman Office, down the pit, to collect the records of the men who had turned up for work. These must have been reports on what was going on that day that Overmen had compiled. On collecting everything, I then ascended the shaft to deliver everything to the undermanager. That was about it! Now and again, there were errands to do such as delivering 'shot' to the shotfirers on the coal face. Well, what a cushy number. How it all ended will be related in part two of my story.

John M Hayes

Part Two
THE FIRST WATERSHED

Chapter One
RELIGION TAKES OVER

The 16th of July 1956—how could one forget the date! As the Evangelicals refer to it—I was 'born again.' How this occurred was really quite bizarre. Once again, and not for the last time, it was due to my dad's influence, though this time inadvertently.

The Derbyshire Times, in the 1950s, would interview someone on the street every week and publish the result in the newspaper; so, it happened that dad was featured one week. This may not have had consequences for him but, indirectly, it certainly did for me. Quite where he got the idea from I'm not sure; all I know is that he told the reporter that his son, John, was going to become a local preacher, and this was printed. Unbeknown to me the piece came to the attention of the young Methodist local preachers, Clifford Booth, Alan Rhodes and George Lord. They decided to make contact to ascertain whether or not I was 'sound.' The three were largely responsible for changing my life, profoundly. One evening, Clifford together with his sister Christine took me to an Evangelical meeting in Sheffield. An Evangelist, Peter Fenwick preached a sermon, working up a sense of guilt about what I now see as normal sexual activity. (How common this was among such preachers, in those days.) Well, I am easily persuaded and was impressionable. (I still am!) In the Billy Graham style, I went forward, responding to the appeal to take Christ as my Saviour. Following a few moments of counselling, that was it! From that day and for the next twenty-four years, I lived in a very different world to that of my family. It became obsessional. Fairly early on, I began to memorise scripture verses. One soon became very personal. The words were from St Paul's letter to the Philippians: FOR ME TO LIVE IS CHRIST AND TO

DIE IS GAIN. Goodness me, how far I'd drifted from the way of life of dad and mam!

An indication of how deeply I'd fallen into this, is that, in the early morning, travelling on the pit bus, I could be found openly reading from a lovely bound edition of the Bible. Eventually, when I was appointed errand boy, I spent time typing out more of the texts I wanted to memorise. One afternoon, as I sat at the tall desk, I sensed Mr Rimmer, the undermanager, was looking at me. Sure enough, Mr Rimmer eventually spoke. "John do you think that you're really suitable for working down the pit?" Soon afterwards, I turned my back on the pit by transferring to work in the time office; hard physical, dangerous work was swapped for a boring clerical job. Unfortunately for the NCB, I wasn't interested any more in a career—my full-time obsession was religion. All other interests or pursuits were abandoned, and now I lived for Christ alone.

Besides attending services every Sunday, I participated in the Chesterfield Youth Squash meetings. People of various Christian denominations were drawn to these Saturday evening meetings, but they were all of an Evangelical persuasion. Particularly, among younger people 'Evangelicals' were found in all of the major Christian Churches in the town, from Pentecostals to Church of England.

Some informal meetings, held in the homes of those who had a hand in running the Youth Squash, took place on an irregular basis. Interestingly, despite being only sixteen, the inner leadership group drew me in to assume some responsibility. Perhaps, it was my serious nature that gave the impression that I was older. Certainly, there could be no one, at the time, more determined to live for Christ and bring more people to him, than John Hayes. It was at one of the house meetings that I first noticed Margaret, one of two sisters. The Staton sisters were well-known and respected. Their church was New Whittington Baptist, a small congregation on the edge of town. This first encounter with them was in our own home, 53 Heathcote Drive.

Sometime later, at one of the meetings in town, I tentatively approached Joyce to reveal a developing interest in her sister. Joyce encouraged me, and this soon led to my walking Margaret to the bus stop where she caught the bus to Matlock. She was a student, training to be a teacher. Eventually, once she had become my girlfriend, I accompanied her on the bus. Very early on in our relationship, I remember feeling over the moon. There is a distinct memory of my sitting on the bus, going home, and thanking God for 'such a treasure.' She was, as I wrote to tell her, just the one I could imagine as my wife. Here was a sixteen-year-old lad relating his feelings to a nineteen-year-old, demonstrating emotional immaturity and impulsiveness, characteristics that remained with me for many, many years.

What originally attracted me to Margaret? First of all, it was her good looks and slim figure. (I've mentioned previously how I was influenced by Hollywood romances—old-fashioned romance was what I was looking for.) We truly fell in love.

Margaret was also a gentle, restrained and kind person, which one could only admire. Again, this conformed to my idea of a perfect wife!

Another significant element in my attraction was Margaret's academic achievements—at school, she had been head girl. I felt it to be a wonderful thing that someone training to be a teacher should be interested in the sixteen-year-old lad, who had left school at fifteen without any qualifications! (Is it altogether surprising that when Margaret told her parents about her sixteen-year-old boyfriend, her mother laughed?)

One of the most important factors in the relationship was a shared faith in Christ. Margaret had been brought up by parents who had become deeply engaged in the church during the early years of marriage. So, it was that when Margaret and I met, she was already committed to 'the faith' (like my own parents, Mr and Mrs Staton were working class—he a railway man, she a sometime factory worker).

Margaret's qualities caused me to place her on a pedestal. Only much later in the relationship did one perceive that idolising a person isn't the firmest foundation on which to build a mature relationship.

I was not the only one to place someone on a pedestal; however, Margaret did the same with me. She sometimes said that she adored me.

Her attraction to me was naturally physical but what impressed her so much was my strong commitment to 'The Lord.'

Bearing in mind the times we lived in before the sixties' sexual revolution, we attempted to abide by the mores of the time—'no sex before marriage.' This was reinforced by religious teaching. It wasn't always easy to be restrained, and how relieved we felt once we were married!

It was, perhaps, through Margaret being a Baptist that influenced me to adopt Baptist thinking, but the most profound influence on my religious development was George Lord. He was, in contrast to Alan Rhodes and Clifford Booth, a hard, judgemental man; sadly, this rubbed off on me. (Interestingly though, his creationist view, as well as those on Hell and the devil, made me feel uneasy from time to time.) As a Methodist local preacher, he presided over Sunday services, and he began to take me with him, sometimes, to give my 'testimony.' These experiences would help to build my confidence in public speaking. The first time I spoke in public about my conversion experience was only a few weeks after the event. George Lord, and others, urged me to talk about it in my own church, Hasland Methodist. So, it was that one Sunday evening, I stood in the pulpit to relate my experiences. So well does the memory of that moment remain, even some of the words said can still be repeated: "When I descend the cage to go down the pit I feel that God is with me." For weeks afterwards, people referred to my 'beaming face.' A Methodist Deaconess spoke openly about 'something having happened to John.'

The other side of the coin, however, was that one became increasingly critical of people in the chapel who didn't appear to have enjoyed a similar experience, that is they were religious but hadn't been 'born again.'

My relationship with Mr & Mrs Slatcher, who had done so much to nurture me, was undermined—it was obvious they were not of an

Evangelical persuasion; they were 'unsound.' Similarly, an encounter with Mr Dale, the tall, gentle church organist, revealed the youthful arrogance and judgemental attitude. Somehow, almost in passing, the subject of Hell arose. Mr Dale couldn't bring himself to believe in a literal Hell, but the difficult sixteen-year-old me was adamant, if one hadn't accepted Christ as Saviour, they were doomed! Poor Mr Dale, he looked so hurt!

Quite clearly, I was increasingly uncomfortable with the Methodists, and before long, left for another church. Before then, however, Christine Booth invited me to see the Scripture Union Group she ran in her church, Storrs Road Methodist. Amazingly, at the age of barely seventeen, and knowing next to nothing about the Bible, I was allowed to start a group in Hasland. How the church leaders allowed this is a mystery to me. The fact that a lot of youngsters turned up must be an indication of how few attractions were available in the village! Quite soon disquiet arose about Scripture Union Notes being promoted. These were very fundamentalist and, understandably, not in favour with Hasland Methodist. It transpired that I was only to be given permission to use some other Bible study notes that were actively promoted by the National Methodist Church. That was asking too much, so I called on the nearby Baptist Church with a view to meeting there. Surprisingly, they made a room available. Some meetings took place, but with the opposition from the Methodists, everything fizzled out. It must have been at about this time that the relationship with Hasland Methodists was severed. Quite soon after attending the Baptist services, I asked to be baptised in the Baptist fashion, that is, by total immersion.

Quite out of the blue, what at first seemed like a disaster for me, dad announced he was leaving the pit to take over a pub—The Middle Club, in Whitwell, a village about ten miles away. I panicked; the move meant that my links with the Christian activity would be slackened. Another issue was the absence of a Baptist Church anywhere near Whitwell. Despite all this, I was obliged to move with the family. The NCB happily found me a job in the time office of Whitwell Colliery.

At the Middle Club, I slept above the bar on the first floor, where the smell of stale beer and smoke put me off both for life! In fact, through religious influence, I was already teetotal, a stance taken until my early thirties. (Even at my wedding, despite dad offering to provide champagne and wine, everyone had to do with apple juice for the toast. Apparently, after Margaret and I left the reception, dad took people for a drink in one of the Chesterfield pubs.)

Ray Cluroe, a family man in his late thirties, worked in the same office as me. Pertinently, he belonged to Portland Street Methodist Church, one of the two Methodist Chapels in the village. One day, he asked me if I'd been 'born again.' It transpired that both he and a small group of others in Whitwell had come under the influence of the Derbyshire Village Mission Sisters, who had spent some months in Whitwell. A small nucleus belonged to the same church as Ray, and it was, perhaps, fortuitous that it was their church that I had started to attend. They were without a leader, and referred to their Minister Rev McKenzie as a 'Modernist.' Incredibly, this individual, completely oblivious of its impact on the mining community, drove around in a Bentley. (His wealthy mother had bought it for him. No doubt, it would have made a different impression on the R.A.F. Station, where he was Chaplain!) The nucleus of 'Bible believers' approached the newly arrived seventeen-year-old to lead a weekly Bible study and prayer meeting. It does seem incomprehensible, especially as my knowledge of the Bible was still extremely limited—it was something like the blind leading the blind.

A mixture of personality, some apparently perceived leadership skills, and, surely, arrogance on my part saw me rise to the challenge! The lack of biblical knowledge was covered up once I'd discovered weekly Bible study lectures from Rev Frank Dixon, Minister of Lansdowne Baptist Church in Bournemouth. These published notes saved the day!

How it started remains unclear but another venture, this time a joint one with the other Methodist Church in the village, saw me leading it. A youth meeting was started. As with the youth meeting I ran in Hasland, a lot of youngsters came along (age group probably eight to thirteen). Several adults volunteered to help. The wonder is that I got away with it; my very limited knowledge became all too obvious to me! All that was on offer from this seventeen/eighteen-year-old was conviction, arrogance and force of personality! Not that the venture lasted for long. Rev McKenzie decided he must intervene to prevent a pernicious germ poisoning his middle-of-the-road complacent congregation. Everything had come to a head through my being given responsibility for planning a youth weekend, for both churches. I'd arranged for some of my Chesterfield friends to take the services. It was, perhaps, unfortunate that I had also arranged for one of this group, prior to the youth weekend, to take one of the regular Sunday evening services. Complaints poured in that the young man had preached on a passage in St Matthew where Jesus lambasted the Pharisees for 'hypocrisy.' The Whitwell congregation felt battered by the preacher's tone: "Hypocrites, Hypocrites!" In no time at all, after receiving disturbing reports, Rev McKenzie stepped in. I was more or less barred from his church; the youth weekend was, of course, taken out of my hands, leaving me stranded.

John M Hayes

Chapter Two
A MARRIED MAN AT NINETEEN

Our marriage was brought forward when Stephen, one of the prayer group people, offered us his furnished cottage for twenty-five shillings a week rent. At the time, my wages from the pit were about £7.00 a week; Margaret, now in the second year of teaching, earned a little more than that. It was a no-brainer to take-up Stephen's offer.

The wedding took place in New Whittington Baptist Church on 19th December 1959. George Lord was the best man; I couldn't think of anyone else to ask! (The lack of male friendship dogged me for many years.)

By this time, a more sympathetic minister, Reverend Hubbard, had taken over from Reverend McKenzie. He welcomed us into the congregation, even encouraging me, at the age of twenty, to become a local preacher on the Worksop Circuit. It really is astonishing, knowing how controlling Methodism was, that without any of the usual training, I was let loose in the village chapels. What was it, the force of personality again? In some ways, I was out of my depth, so much so that one good sermon was preached over and over again! Visiting mainly small chapels where there were usually only a handful of people present, I nevertheless enjoyed the experience very much. The pulpit seemed my natural habitat. One received no expenses, but this was sometimes compensated for in the form of delicious lunches and/or teas. A humorous though, at the time, painful event comes to mind. An 'evangelical' couple in one of the small outlying villages provided hospitality for the day. The young man collected me on his motorbike, in time for morning service. Afterwards, we retired to his house where his domestic science teacher wife provided a feast her guest would never forget! At lunch, the first course was a traditional, massive Yorkshire pudding. This was followed by meat and lots of vegetables. The only drawback was that I had contracted a heavy cold, so, on puddings being served, the lunch became unforgettable for me. Unfortunately, more was to come; at tea time, it was like going back in time with Grandma Knowles. The hostess was truly a wonderful baker, and she had determined to impress! How I survived the service and the ride back home, I have no idea; I certainly felt ill!

At home, on some Sunday evenings, a small number of young people assembled. Unsurprisingly, the intention was to 'lead them to Christ,' and, in this regard, some success transpired.

Throughout this time, Margaret continued to teach full time. I worked four different weekly shifts in the Time Office. Work was only a few minutes cycle-ride away. Many afternoons would see me cycling around the flat country where I would often stop at a small Parish Church to say prayers. One, especially remembered, is a lovely church where the Duchess of Portland worshipped. Hopefully, she wouldn't have minded that a young keen Christian man sometimes used her engraved prayer book. Prayer now featured greatly; I was a deeply spiritual man, aspiring to realise a personal relationship 'with the Lord.' This lay at the very heart of everything. As far as it is possible to discover, my intensity was, perhaps, unique among the group of friends or acquaintances. Was it then inevitable that one day found me telling Margaret that I felt God was calling me to be a missionary? It was no surprise to me that Margaret offered her total support! Having left school at fifteen, a vague feeling left me with the thought that some further education would be required. Reverend Ridyard, a Baptist Minister acquaintance in Retford, had studied at The Glasgow Bible College, and so, it was that the idea of studying at that institution arose. Reverend Ridyard, who in his time had been head student, eagerly encouraged me to apply. Reverend Hubbard also indicated his full support should I apply. In the end, an application went ahead; it was accepted. We could now anticipate two years where I'd be a student at Glasgow Bible College, 64 Bothwell Street, a grim dirty Victorian building, half of which was the YMCA.

Everything was almost wrecked for our plans when Margaret became pregnant, with the birth due in November, that is during my first term in college. It had been the intention that Margaret would support us for two years by teaching in a Glasgow school. That plan having now been scuppered, we fell back on what we knew as the Hudson Taylor approach. This man had founded the China Inland Mission in Victorian times. Not believing in begging for financial support, his mantra was "God will provide." Taylor was one of our idols, and we gave financial support to the mission (now renamed The Overseas Missionary Fellowship [OMF]).

Before moving to Glasgow, we attended a large conference of the society at The Hayes in Swanwick. (It was there that we met Mr & Mrs Guiness who were the OMF representatives in Glasgow, of all the places.)

So, it was with the naïve faith that we confidently made plans for the move to Glasgow.

Chapter Three
THE COLLEGE YEARS

Because the baby was expected in November, it was thought best if Margaret stayed with her parents to have the birth in Chesterfield, whilst I spent the first term in college. This arrangement would give me time to find accommodation for us in Glasgow.

In September 1961, therefore, Margaret, together with her sister Joyce, saw me off at Chesterfield Station, taking the lunchtime 'Thames Clyde Express.' This is the train I often 'spotted' during the lunch break at Peter Webster School. What an exciting sight, a double-headed train, usually two impressive Jubilee Class locomotives, belching out plumes of smoke with steam escaping from several parts! For me, now to be travelling on this train seemed surreal. Never before had I taken such a long journey. The journey seemed endless, but I was enchanted as we steamed along the Settle to Carlisle scenic route (a line saved from closure that now attracts tourists). Scenery in the Scottish Borders quite overwhelmed me; never before had I seen such natural beauty. My emotional response to seeing it all was profound. Oh, what a world was out there, one day to be explored!

Our journey, on the other hand, provided some disconcerting moments. Unsurprisingly, lots of Scots were on the train; their strong accents were baffling—would I ever be able to understand what the Glaswegians were saying? Long before Glasgow, some of them caused me to feel uncomfortable as they had patently imbibed a lot of alcohol. Drunkenness had always caused me to feel frightened; a drunk can be so unpredictable! Fortunately, another very different experience took my mind off the trouble. A young lad engaged me in conversation. After hearing about the adventure I was embarking on, he asked me a series of questions. As the train finally approached its destination, the lad told me that he knew where Bothwell Street was; he very kindly offered to escort me and even to carry my case! This was the first experience of Glaswegian warmth, and it proved to be reassuring.

The college had been established by Moody and Sankey, two American evangelists in the nineteenth century. It was open to members of all Protestant denominations throughout the world. What a stimulating experience for a working-class lad to be surrounded by scores of students from many nations! In the first week, a 'testimony' session took place, when each student gave an account of how they became a Christian. For me, this was overwhelming—to quote my diary, which I had begun to keep, *"it melted my heart."*

A rather sad contrast was when I came to realise one student, a Bill Fearnehough from Sheffield, was the son of a steel magnet for whom Aunty Mable used to cook. Bill was rather aloof when I made him aware of our connection. He always gave the impression of being above the likes of me. No doubt, this would only help to feed my warped view of the 'upper class,' and of private education.

Living in college for a term meant I was obliged to do chores, like washing and ironing, for the first time! One was there, however, to work hard on study, which for a fifteen-year-old school leaver was far from easy. Embarrassment arose when my poor spelling and paucity of vocabulary became obvious. I came up with the idea of writing lists of words I wanted to learn to spell; then, another idea arose to compile a vocabulary list. These lists were written on postcards, which fitted into a top jacket pocket, so they could be referred to at odd moments, for example, when taking a bus to college. Throughout the years, I've continued to do this in one way or another. Now, I'm quite proud of my improvement.

Studies consisted of biblical texts, theology and church history, primarily. One part-time lecturer, on church history, was extremely charismatic. Once he told us, "The educated man is not necessarily one who knows so much but rather one who knows where to find the knowledge whenever it is required." What fun his lessons were!

Another Church of Scotland Minister came in to lecture us on the Old Testament; he also was quite fun. In contrast to these two, was Mr Grogan, a lecturer in theology. He was an intensely serious character but gentle and kind. The principal, Reverend Andrew McBeath, began each morning lecturing on the New Testament. Another caring man, who often shared news of former students who had written to him.

To those, like me, with little education and few, if any, qualifications, the college offered classes for 'O' and 'A' levels, as well as a Certificate in Religious Education from London University. A former Eton man introduced me to Shakespeare, first with Twelfth Night, which I found bewildering, then with Henry The Fifth. This difference reflected my preference for the serious and my disdain for the frivolous! Although in later life, my second wife Maggie, an English graduate, endeavoured to assure me that 'Twelfth Night' should be taken seriously.

Very early on, I struggled with New Testament (NT) Greek. On 10th October, a diary entry reads:

"Unfortunately, it looks as if I shall have to discontinue Greek, as I'm rather in a cloud; I'm disappointed, but won't worry."

Besides studies, students were expected to engage in practical evangelistic work in one of four areas of the city. Having a somewhat romantic tendency, I opted for the notorious slum-infested Gorbals. (Just a few years previously, the police had cleared out violent gangs but some dangers persisted.)

Our group leader was Klaus Mahler, a very serious German, who once corrected me by saying, "you should learn to think before you speak!" (In all the subsequent years, I often recalled this, and at the same time, regretted not taking any notice of it!) Work in the Gorbals centred around one of the lesser sects of the Church of Scotland. The minister was a hospitable sort—we sometimes met his family over a meal. On one occasion, hearing noises from upstairs, we were informed it was a seriously deformed, mentally ill daughter of the family. She was brought down to share tea. Seeing her was quite a shock, but it increased my admiration for the parents who were determined not to have her locked away and out of sight.

Students working in the area of this church sometimes attended Sunday morning service. As for myself, once Margaret and baby Andrew had joined me in Glasgow, we decided to worship as a family at Adelaide Place Baptist Church, a very different city church. Reverend George Young, who had served in China, was the renowned minister. We were officially welcomed into the membership of this church.

In the Gorbals, our work centred around a young peoples' club. Meetings took place every week—the aim being 'to lead them to Christ.' One amazing weekend, we took some of them to a Christian conference centre on the bank of the Clyde. (For me, the spectacular landscape proved to be awe-inspiring.)

This was another impact of going to Scotland; it reinforced a profound awe and, at the same time, delight in the countryside—something, once again, that had been absent in my family. In the last week at the Bible Training Institute (BTI), the whole college was taken on an amazing train journey—it must have been on the line from Glasgow to Fort William that we came to know well in later years. I never forgot the impact of the mountains. Another outdoor trip took place in the first term. On Tuesday, 21st October 1961, a group of us set off to climb Ben Ime. Although the weather forced a retreat before we reached the peak, it was a "glorious" experience for me.

Diary Entry:
"To be able to get into the fresh air and enjoy the glory and beauty of creation is a wonderful thing."

(It is interesting that in 1981, sometime after I embraced atheism, it was walking in the lovely countryside near Chesham that, temporarily, reawakened in me a faith in some kind of God!)

As I was writing these pages, I read extracts from my very first personal diary, started on the eve of the Glasgow adventure. What I read shocked me! I had forgotten some of the terrible guilt and depression suffered. On an undated entry, but sometime in September 1961, I'd written the following:

Diary Entry: September 1961

"Very busy day packing and preparing to move. Felt rather nervous regarding college. I have need to be when I think of my state spirituality."

Although delighted to be at Glasgow Bible College, almost devastating guilt was never far away.

Diary Entry: 12th October 1961

"The more I go on, the more I feel I agree with God's verdict on the human heart."

"Desperately wicked and deceitful above all things" and then "I am so self-centred."

I was predominantly thinking of myself in my studies and even in practical work, which is why, sometimes, I found it a strain.

Diary Entry:

"How the devil likes to get us grumbling, complaining over little things. It is that which destroys our peace and sense of God's presence."

Diary Entry: 19th October

"I'm so anxious, tho[ugh], of so much sin and failure."

Wow! What is it that made me feel so self-condemnatory, nothing more than deep-seated insecurity, due to failure to realise a totally unrealistic aspiration—that is the aspiration to be a saint !

Here is yet another self-condemnatory entry—and I'd only been in Glasgow for a few weeks.

Diary Entry: 23rd October

"I'm up and down quite a lot, but I'm pressing on, seeking to look away from myself to the Lord. Oh if any man knew my heart, whatever would they think? I know what St Paul felt like when he called himself 'The chief of sinners!'"

Quite clearly, I was very self-centred! This state of mind arose out of a fanatical approach to religion. It led to a neglect of and a lack of interest in other people, even the family. It is no doubt significant that the first diary mention of 'Andrew,' who was born on 16th November, wasn't made until 4th December, two and a half weeks later! Even then, the reference was skewed by my ultra and guilt-ridden approach to life.

Diary Entry: 4th December

"May he grow up to be a true 'Andrew'—a fisher of men, pointing others to the Saviour."

Patently, religion had produced a contradictory emotional state; at times, it gave me a firm sense of purpose, even joy, then, on the other hand, guilt, dissatisfaction and depression.

This conflict, often intense, was to last until the age of forty, when, finally, renouncing religion, I chose atheism and experienced release. At that time, or very soon afterwards, Rachel, our eldest daughter, said, "Dad you are much less tense these days!"

Before Margaret came to join me in Glasgow, we corresponded daily. The letters as well as diary entries reveal a powerful emotional bond. They also reveal my naive and somewhat distorted view of a marriage relationship.

Diary Entry: 23rd September

"Praise the Lord for my dear sweetheart. I do praise the Lord for my sweetheart. She is such a simple soul—oh and how I love her, not in a base way, but sweetly and fervently. She is the darling of my heart, the fairest of ten thousand. I wish every man had such a treasure as mine."

Diary Entry: 21st October

"My darling wife is constantly on my mind. I do love her so much—what a priceless treasure she is."

How one could have felt so very differently, within a year, is another story! At this time, however, I put her on a pedestal—she was a good person, devoted first to God, secondly to me. What I failed to spot is that she was already living through me, which was dangerous.

Through college, I grew and developed quickly—she stood still! This was the beginning of an alienation.

Andrew was born on 16th November. Although I was down in time, my dad was the first person to know. He drove over to my in-laws to break the news. Andrew had been delivered with forceps. Margaret stayed in hospital for a few days. Andrew was a lovely-looking baby, quite obviously a Hayes! I returned to complete the first college term, before spending time in Chesterfield over Christmas, and afterward taking Margaret and Andrew to Glasgow.

Fairly soon after I arrived in Glasgow, I found a basement flat that we would all occupy from 2nd January. Long before going to college, both Margaret and I had become supporters of the China Inland Mission, later to be renamed 'The Overseas Missionary Fellowship.' On discovering that a weekly prayer meeting was held in their Glasgow HQ, I joined a few other students in attending. My diary entry reads:

"Study is hard when one is not accustomed to it. I had a headache too and didn't feel inclined to go to the CIM prayer meeting."

Diary Entry:

"Glad I went. Mr Guiness told me they had a flat to rent, and we could have it."

Then, there are references to how good God is!

Diary Entry:

"We knew he would provide, yet didn't imagine, it would be either so soon or so pleasant. Praise to the Lord."

Some weeks later, further evidence of this provision came in the form of a letter.

Margaret and I had gone to college without financial resources but were convinced God would look after us. Originally, the idea was that Margaret would earn money teaching but that idea was knocked on the head when she became pregnant! We decided to obey the call and trust in the Lord. Our attitude was influenced by one of our heroes,

Hudson Taylor, founder of the China Inland Missionwho never directly appealed for money but trusted in God to provide. To many of our friends, even the Christian ones, it seemed a crazy idea, but before the end of my first term at the BTI, the looked-for miracle was delivered. Having previously had a request for a Derbyshire Council Grant refused, on account of my having left school at fifteen, and therefore not sporting any academic qualifications, it was a surprise when I received an invitation for an interview. It transpired, not for the first time, that my dad had taken a hand in determining my fate.

This time, dad was running the Middle Club in Whitwell, and he decided to speak about me to the local County Councillor, who was one of his regulars. I can well imagine how it went. "Aye up so and so, my lad's gone to college, and 'they' won't give him a grant." The first thing I knew of it was when a letter arrived at college inviting me to an interview with the Director of Education's Deputy, in the Christmas holidays, when we would be staying with Margaret's family. Jack Longland was a highly respected Director of Education and a nationally renowned Broadcaster. Wow, was this how God was going to provide? That is certainly how we took it when, shortly after the interview, a grant, backdated to September and fixed for two years, arrived in the post. What else could it be but confirmation that we were doing God's Will.

Rather foolishly, the three of us took the train to Glasgow on 2nd January 1962. Being ignorant of so much, we had not anticipated most of Glasgow's taxi drivers being off work, no doubt recovering from the excesses of Hogmanay! To make matters worse, Glasgow was shrouded in a 'peasouper' fog. I was very concerned about our young baby. When we finally arrived at Hillhead Avenue, Mrs Guiness greeted us with the news that the few sticks of furniture that we'd sent by rail had not arrived—yet, another casualty of Hogmanay. Mary and Henry, however, provided the warmest of welcomes, and a good night's sleep was enjoyed in a bed they had made up. Next day, all turned out well, and Henry and Mary's son, Oswald, who also attended the BTI, gave us a hand with the goods and chattels. The basement flat was quite dark, but we had plenty of room—three very large rooms, in fact. There we were until June, when we returned to Chesterfield for the summer. One reason for the return was because a job, in the Town Hall, had been offered for the duration of the college break at £10.00 per week.

Despite being comfortably set up for my second term, the seeds were sown for some challenges, which arose in the second college year. The first doubts about Christian beliefs emerged but not as yet very strongly. Then, perhaps, because I was spending whole days and even evenings at college, the marriage relationship deteriorated. Looking back, it seems that I selfishly allowed myself to milk the stimulation of college whilst Margaret was left, in the flat, to go stale. It was certainly the case that one can see in hindsight that Margaret was doing little for herself, and I was neglecting her. Certainly, at the weekends, we enjoyed Kelvin Park and the beautiful botanical gardens, but even when at home, I would shut Margaret out to pursue study. That came first, i.e., I came first!

Without being aware of it, Margaret, as my dear Spurgeon's friend Peter said, many, many years later, "Margaret lived for and through you." Sadly, this was something that I, unconsciously, connived with. I did not work on our relationship, and to compound matters, Margaret was very much confined by the baby whilst I was having a rare old time making new relationships, enjoying many interesting experiences. My days were full, hers were largely empty! To be honest with myself, perhaps, the truth is, Margaret was beginning to seem boring to me but that was very much due to my neglect of her and Andrew. Sadly, as I developed intellectually, she stagnated. This was a major reason for our growing apart. Undoubtedly, being unable to converse on the same level became a conscious weakness of the marriage. I felt frustrated and lonely.

What is shocking is that when I went back to the diary to see what was written there, I found no entries after 23rd February. Was I already unconsciously harbouring disillusions? Certainly, matters deteriorated during the second college year. I will come back to that, but first, a significant experience occurred between the two college years.

John M Hayes

Like many students in those days, I applied for a summer job in the Town Hall, Chesterfield. Again, financial provision seemed to be assured when I was appointed to assist the Borough Street Lighting Engineer. It transpired that the previous summer, two students had been appointed to work on a special project of his. Mr Jones, who lived close to the Town Hall and professed to be a Roman Catholic, turned out to be somewhat of a fraud. Other people in the Engineering Department told me Mr Jones' job had only recently been devised. Previously, anything to do with street lighting had been allocated to any one of the teams. It was on the very first day that it dawned on me that Mr Jones only wanted a student in his office so that he could cover his tracks. On greeting me, he started to chat, and then suggested, we had a cup of tea. After about half an hour, he explained that he would be out of the office all day. I was left sitting behind a large desk with nothing but a telephone on it; Mr Jones asked me to make a note of any calls. There may have been two or three messages for him when he turned up again about 4.30 p.m. Over another cup of tea, I asked what he would like me to do next day. "Haven't you any books to read?" was his retort. Quite shocked, I eventually stumbled over an answer. The procedure from that time was that I got well paid for pursuing study. In the meantime, it was obvious Mr Jones was 'skiving.' When he had any genuine appointment, which was not often, he would mention it, so it was obvious he was cheating on the days nothing specific was being done. In fact, on a walkabout one lunchtime, I spotted his car outside his house; one could only assume that his car was parked there for much of the time he was being paid to do some work. People working in Town Halls these days assured me that things have changed drastically, but Mr Jones was employed at a time of empire building, inefficiency and waste in the public sector.

During the second college year, the seeds of destruction of both my marriage and faith were sown. I had been elected by my peers to lead the Gorbals team, i.e., the students who were to work together in the Gorbals area. (The appointment surprised me, but it was once again confirmed that some people believed that I demonstrated leadership ability.) Within days of term starting, the new students had been allocated to one of four teams. Our Gorbals team met for introductions. Following the meeting, Elaine Berry approached me, glowing with enthusiasm at the prospect of working in the Gorbals. She spoke about her determination to support my leadership. That was almost a defining moment; here was an Oxbridge Classical Scholar, expressing respect for me. Personally, it was like a trap door had been opened into which I eventually fell.

Praise and flattery led me astray, not only at that moment, but also many times throughout the years. My insecurity led me to lay too much store on praise and recognition.

On the academic level, I'd received some encouragement by obtaining, from London University, a Certificate of Religious Knowledge. By now, I was considering a future in the Ministry of the Baptist Church. During the summer, we had participated in a children's mission at the seaside. (Interestingly, dad had driven up to see us in Glasgow, and he helpfully transported us to the coast. I wasn't sure what he made of the frugal fare he shared with the Children's Special Service Mission in the large, rented house in which we were billeted!)

On the beach, one day, we met two Baptist Church ministers, who were on holiday. One was a minister in Gray's Baptist Church, Essex, and the other in the Dagenham Group of Churches. This latter man was also on the Council of Spurgeon's College. Inevitably, this just about persuaded me that I should eventually apply to enter this college. Spurgeon's was situated in Norwood, South London. The building was a former mansion given to Charles Haddon Spurgeon, the most famous preacher in mid-Victorian times. Eventually, the application to the college was submitted. When notice was given of an interview, which included a basic test on NT Greek, in my panic, Elaine Berry came to the rescue. She had qualified in Classics, and NT Greek was not so different from the ancient language she was familiar with. Somehow, a copy of the short Greek piece used in previous tests at Spurgeon's came into my possession. Elaine perused this and used it as a benchmark for my tuition. Learning the language didn't come easy for me; I struggled. Nevertheless, the assistance given to me did make all the difference. My problem was that I'd never even understood the basic grammar of English, never mind that of another language. Apart from the alphabet, everything about NT Greek seemed confusing, chaotic and totally beyond comprehension.

My work in the Gorbals was certainly engrossing; I saw a side of life one would never have known existed. The BTI students often worked in pairs, with one of each sex. Residents of the slums were visited, and there were some regulars on the visiting itinerary. One early evening, having climbed the stairs up several storeys of a tenement, we knocked on the door of a young family we knew. The husband had a regular job as a bricklayer but couldn't find a rented house outside the Gorbals. (At this time, Glasgow Corporation had started to rehouse some Gorbals residents, but the majority of people were still stuck in the slums.)

Having knocked on the door, a man's voice was heard, "can you wait a minute, she's in the bath." The lady of the house was having, what was presumably, her weekly bath in front of the roaring coal fire. Eventually, the door opened to us, and we were greeted like old friends and shared a pot of tea. (One thing always impressed me—how open and friendly Gorbals residents were to us.)

There was another occasion, after spending an hour or so in the area, Elaine and I were on our way back to the college when a man accosted us. "Is that a Bible?" he asked me. "Yes," I replied. His response was to ask us if we would call on his wife. "She's locked me out. Can you persuade her to let me in?" There was obviously a crisis, so the decision was made to visit the woman to see if there was any help we could give.

Having rung the doorbell and waited, we then realised that whoever was at home was observing us through a spy hole. On explaining what we were doing there, we were let in by the wife. What a sight greeted us! The apartment was just one huge room. Part of it was occupied by a gigantic bed, where it was explained that the couple and their two young children slept. There was a communal toilet on the stairs.

Once again, out came the teapot! How is it that the poor can be so hospitable and generous?

Then, out poured the story. The husband was an alcoholic (Glasgow was full of such). Having just returned from rehabilitation, he'd gone straight back onto the drink. "I can't have him back. It's not safe for the children."

There was, of course, nothing to be done. On returning to meet the husband, we found he had disappeared into thin air, or more likely, into one of the numerous pubs. (Almost every street corner of the area had what I referred to as a 'gin shop,' which the Catholic nuns visited once a week to collect alms!)

One Sunday morning, after joining the morning service in the Gorbals Church, two of us decided to visit one of our 'contact' families. On our arrival, the small family were just about to eat lunch. (Tatties and gravy. Reminiscent of the Irish famine days!) We didn't stay long. The husband, either through disability or laziness, was 'out of work.' His wife kept the family, through night work on the streets! Such was life in the Gorbals!

We often met a mentally sick man, around 40ish and who always wore a distinctive coat, perhaps, picked up in a charity shop; he once took us to see his apartment. It was on the top floor, in a dilapidated state; the plaster ceiling was partly missing so the lattice work was exposed. It was conditions such as these that quietly but surely drew me into a socialist view. Certainly, the poor in Glasgow appeared to have been ground down and left to rot. But one also came to observe another side of the coin—some individuals were their own worst enemy. Drink was most certainly a destroyer of family life, and worse, it was a killer. Wherever we were walking in the city, alcoholics would approach us for money. College authorities strongly advised against giving money, although a drink, with a bite, might be acceptable. One evening, again on walking back to college, a man approached to ask if I would give him the little Bible I usually carried around with me.

The Bible was of sentimental value, but I offered to find him a Bible if he walked with me back to the college. Of course, on reaching the college steps, it immediately became clear that the man wasn't at all interested in a Bible. On being asked to wait outside, whilst I went to find a Bible for him, he cursed and swore. The poor chap received nothing to buy more liquor with!

One dark, damp winter evening about 5 p.m., walking innocently along a pavement, a tall man, obviously drunk, took out a knife to me; before I had time to panic, another man intervened and pushed me aside, saying "run for it." Such was life in the Glasgow Gorbals!

As the Spurgeon's interview drew near, I became almost emotionally dependent on Elaine. She did not merely work hard on my Greek tuition but, much more importantly, boosted my confidence, my self-esteem. She affirmed me. This had the negative effect of me developing an unhealthy dependence. She was not an attractive woman; it was not the body I'd found attractive but it was the mind—the enthusiastic, vibrant personality. Looking back, I can see that the friendship fed my hunger for recognition and appreciation. I just couldn't believe that such a highly intelligent and extremely well-educated person could value and like me! Unfortunately, the emotional dependence had the tendency to alienate me from Margaret. At the beginning of the college day, all the students assembled for a session from the principal. I would sit in the lecture theatre, deliberately anticipating seeing Elaine enter.

This new experience was a shock to me. It was totally unexpected. But it was too late; the damage had been done. What had caused this infatuation revealed the limitations of the marriage. Although Margaret and I were genuinely in love, there was a lack of intimacy, not sexually, but emotionally. Margaret was shy, and this could only have been reinforced by the isolation and loneliness. A letter she sent me some years later said it all. *"Lately, you've asked me if I minded you staying at college. It depends what you mean. If you mean do I care that you are not home often—of course I do. When tea-time comes round, I begin to feel quite lost and find myself wandering to the window to see if* you are coming down the road. I am always glad when I hear your whistle as you mount the stairs.

Should you mean, do I mind—as resentful. No, no, no! The first summer at the BTI when you did your first GCEs (General Certificate of Education) and spent almost all your time at college, I did find it hard and had often to pray for the Lord's help. The battle over that sort of minding was won then and I could leave you happily to study most days because it's the Lord's work you are on."

The poignancy of this epistle didn't seem obvious at the time, but that is the point, I had become self-absorbed, and at the same time, less loving, less caring towards Margaret. Unfortunately, as I believe her letter showed, Margaret tended to what my dearest male friend said, "to live through me." Frankly, she didn't think enough of herself; she didn't speak up for herself! I was ashamed of the ensuing alienation and felt trapped. Despite the shame, my selfish behaviour never changed, I continued to take advantage of her submission.

Nothing physical ever took place with Elaine—not even a word was uttered about my emotions. But feelings were so dominant, they almost took over my daily thoughts. Elaine, I discovered years later, hadn't a clue about this, and she, herself, was completely innocent.

At home, despite our shared faith, we were uncomfortable even praying together—in fact, we abandoned the attempt. I've mentioned Margaret's shyness, but it must have been also my own underdeveloped emotional life. For instance, I was unable to pick up baby Andrew to cuddle! The only intimacy I was comfortable with was sexual. Natural warmth took decades to arise in me. It's now so, so much easier with the young grandchildren. So, there were personality deficiencies on both sides. There did come a time in the early 70s when a breakthrough occurred, but it was not sufficient in itself to make a lasting difference.

One other important development took place at this time. A former Eton and Oxbridge man was the most fundamentalist of the lecturers. In one 'special' lecture, he strove to reconcile some of the Old Testament inconsistencies. To a person who believes that every word of the Bible was more or less dictated by God, the actual text presents huge challenges. Accordingly, some scholars go into contortions to reconcile the 'apparent' inconsistencies. But, even at this stage in development, and in such a hot bed of fundamentalism, I really wasn't comfortable with this approach.

More seriously, for perhaps only brief moments, I almost lost faith in Christianity altogether. One day, kneeling in the flat to say my prayers, an involuntary thought entered my head: "I wonder if I'm just talking to the ceiling." It came like an electric shock but disturbed me to realise that, even if only momentarily, I could doubt even the very existence of God!

Perhaps, it was the growing recognition that our 'clients' in the Gorbals would never become Christ's disciples; their attitudes, culture and experience militated against it. This realisation helped to sow the seeds of doubts. There would also have been the usual challenges of faith to face up to—especially the problem of pain and general suffering—and what about all the different religions, and even the numerous Christian groups? (The Church of Scotland, over time, experienced at least four breakaway groups!) Confronting life in a city slum began to have an impact on how I saw life, its meaning and purpose. But, not to exaggerate this, on my subsequent application to Spurgeon's, I owned up to a belief in 'the verbal inspiration of Scripture.' The interviews and test at Spurgeon's took place in the early spring. On the very first day, and even before entering the hallowed precincts, a tremendously significant encounter took place.

At the Elephant and Castle, I caught a double-decker bus, number 68, for South Norwood, and I made for the top deck. It was there that I bumped into a man who became and remained the closest male friend I've ever had—Peter Edwards from Wallasey. He was on his way to Spurgeon's. Having completed National Service in the Royal Air Force, where he was 'converted' and baptised, he felt a call by God to become a minister. As I'll elaborate on later, we were very different personalities—all I'll say here is Peter was one of the kindest, most generous people one could meet.

The exams took place, as did the interview, which involved a room full of men assessing the candidates. Sometime before, I was warned that someone may say to me "What will you do if your application is rejected?" My retort was to say, "I'll say that I'll reapply the following year." (I'm not sure this question did arise, but my words illustrate the abounding confidence I had in God's calling.) Well, indeed, confirmation of a college place arrived, post-haste.

During our time in Glasgow, we were able to join Adelaid Place Baptist Church. It had a building of some grandeur with stone pillars—perhaps, the architecture was influenced by the massive Spurgeon's Tabernacle in the Elephant and Castle, London. Reverend George Young was kind to us and was the guest preacher at my Ordination service in Doncaster in 1967. George Young also supported my application for Spurgeon's, though he didn't know us well. Apart from joining his congregation, there was little involvement—I hadn't much free time.

Glasgow had a concert venue, The Kelvin Hall, very close to Hillhead Street. Elaine Berry, who knew a lot about classical music, offered to babysit so that Margaret and I could attend a concert. Another pivotal experience, my first live concert! The programme was Rachmaninov's 2nd Piano Concerto, followed by Tchaikovsky's 5th Symphony. For many years, it was impossible for us to visit a concert hall—I couldn't afford a ticket! But once again, a seed had been sown that years later grew into a passion for such music, and when the financial situation afforded, to attending many, many concerts and listening at home to many recordings.

When Elaine asked me what was being performed, she exclaimed, "Oh very romantic!" What she didn't realise is that, although I'd never heard it or ever heard of the pieces before, they went right into my heart; it is music that can move one deeply. Significantly, these two pieces of music became, and, to this day, remain two of my favourites. The composers, two of my all-time favourites too!

We moved to Chesterfield for the summer. Mr Jones was still around, and again, I made it possible for him to 'work' from home!

John M Hayes

Chapter Four
ALL SET FOR A UNIVERSITY EDUCATION

Cheekily, I applied to the County Council for another grant but was given short shrift. However, I was invited to apply once again the following year, when it was anticipated I could begin working for a Bachelor of Divinity Degree from London University to which Spurgeon's College was affiliated.

The first challenge was finding somewhere to live, but despite searching, I had to start studies by living in college, as had happened in Glasgow. Within a very short time, however, something did turn up in Knolly's Road, Streatham. One flat was on the first floor where we shared a toilet with a friendly couple on the second floor. By now, Margaret was heavily pregnant, expecting a birth in late November.

I was one of the very first married men to enrol at the college. The tutors were totally unprepared for dealing with married men. The obvious public school setup was about to be seriously challenged. Although there were one or two other married students in my 'batch,' the faculty had made no provision for such a radical change. Perhaps, not surprisingly, because apart from Mr Rusling, the history tutor, not one of them was able to provide any needed pastoral care for their charges. For myself, being cut off from a church for four years, and therefore not having a pastor I could talk to, this failing of the faculty had a profoundly negative impact on me.

On graduating, after four years, I unkindly spoke to the principal about it. I shocked him by saying that I was leaving the college a bitter, resentful person. Although it was my own doing, couldn't it have been a different story if a pastoral care system had been available in Spurgeon's?

Life at Knolly's Road was comfortable enough. Sometimes lying in bed, we heard the couple upstairs having, what sounded like, very exciting sex! Were we missing something? This couple were lovely though, and when in November, Margaret went to King's College Hospital for the birth of our baby, they kindly offered to care for Andrew so that I could accept the hospital's invitation to be present at the birth. Being squeamish and lacking so much in confidence, both offers were declined. Roger was born on 30th November; he and Margaret were to spend a few days in the hospital as was wont in those days. Rob Riden, a fellow student, had a small car, and he generously acted as chauffeur to bring them home. Each lunchtime, I'd feed Andrew, who was now two years old, on cheese and apple. When Margaret, on seeing Andrew, commented on his rosy cheeks, I felt justified! In reality, I knew nothing about cooking, apart from making beans on toast and tomatoes on toast and boiling an egg! Neither did I know a thing about how to care for a two-year-old.

In the few days I was resident in college, before we had the flat, I was able to meet our 'Batch,' all sixteen of us. Some were as intense about their religion as me. An example was Philip Greenslade, fresh from university. Dapper, good looking, short, neat and highly intelligent, Philip was extremely intense. My diary records "I've had a time of fellowship and prayer with Philip. It would not surprise me if he does not turn out to be the spiritual friend I have desired for years." (David Fawcett, at the BTI, agreed on 4th December to spend fifteen minutes together in prayer, but this, inevitably, ceased once I was no longer living in college.)

The day after the covenant with Philip, the principal gave the batch a pep talk. Immediately afterwards, we agreed to meet weekly for prayer and fellowship. Really, I suppose we covenanted to keep together to be delivered from the particular temptations of theological college life. Such was the original intensity and determination! (For some reason, however, neither my covenant with Philip nor the agreement of the batch was fulfilled.) How easy it was to make impetuous decisions! Gradually, an awareness grew that I was the most impetuous individual. Remembering Klaus Mahler's exhortation to "think before you speak," only seemed like a slight break on this tendency of mine!

From the outset, my priority was to study. Many of the other students already held a university degree, which meant they were going to find study straightforward. It was this commitment that motivated my working in the college library some Saturday mornings, leaving Margaret alone again. On one of these Saturday mornings, an extremely significant encounter took place, which in part revealed my propensity to be critical and judgemental. There was certainly an arrogance in what I did that morning. I was in the junior common room when Gustov Khan (a blind student) arrived very upset, complaining about the absence of pastoral care, which made my blood boil! Already, it was apparent that Spurgeon's wasn't a patch on the BTI when it came to supporting people. At the BTI, students were addressed by their first name. At Spurgeon's, it was always 'Mr'; they called it showing respect. I called it public school formality and reserve. Once again acting impetuously, I ran to the house where Mr Fitzsimmons, the New Testament tutor lived. For ages, I was with him, speaking too freely as it transpired. On the following Monday morning, I was called into the staff room. What a dressing down occurred; I felt humiliated. Almost in tears, I left with my tail between my legs! The seed of resentment had been sown, which subsequently grew into a deadly plant, strangling my joy and distorting my reason. Already, one was rudely awakened to the painful reality, that being in a theological college did not mean everyone treated one another with respect and kindness. Oh dear! Was this another challenge to my faith? Was this Christianity thing real or was it all a hoax?

One thing that was really enjoyable and beneficial was study. Due to not having sufficient 'O' and 'A' levels, the principal recommended that I take 'Greek Literature in Translation' for 'O' level, and I'd already chosen 'English 19th Century Social History' for 'A' level.

Throughout the next four years, history became almost a passion. (For the degree, I chose two history papers and performed well in each, in fact, so well in Historical Theology, that it got me through, according to the principal.) The study of history had a profound influence on my political views. Of course, all my extended family adopted a form of socialism, and now, I joined the club. (It later transpired that only a handful of students and one faculty member voted labour.) Already, study was having a profound effect on my view of the meaning and purpose of life. This was my kind of serious stuff!

Other studies pursued were New and Old Testaments, Theology and, a very limited, one lecture a week on the practical work of a Baptist Minister. The study of Hebrew was undertaken, at first, but after acquiring the ability to read the Hebrew text of 'The Book of Jonah,' this was abandoned in favour of the much more appropriate subject for me, of 'Modern Church History (c1840-1939).' It has to be said that I devoured all this knowledge.

In the meantime, Margaret and I found a church where we could worship together. It was Norwood Baptist Church, a thriving congregation with a distinctive, attractive building and a slightly eccentric, although sincere and respected, minister—Frank Goodwin. Having a creche made it possible for the whole family to be present together. The downside turned out to be that for many Sundays, if not most, I was obliged to take services and preach in other churches. Students were allocated a church that could be fairly local, or many miles away, like Chichester, for example. So once again, it was more isolation for Margaret. Fortunately, she did make some friends, particularly in the Young Wives Group, and they were very kind to us. But how long those Sundays when we were apart must have been. She was, once again, largely living through me!

At this time, we were trying to live frugally. Apart from family allowance (now for two children), no income was being received. Some of the grant received at the BTI had been surplus to our needs, and it was this that supported us. A fellow student, however, Trevor, and his wife Christine, started to give us sporadic, small, but welcome, amounts of money out of the salary Christine was earning. (This was one of the significant examples of generosity shown to us over all the years in the church; and it had come completely unexpectedly.) Another and even more significant income came from a share of the fees we students received on Sundays from churches where we conducted the services. Almost every week, the monies would be handed out following a common room after lunch session. Speaking of taking services, our grocery bill was helped by the lunches and teas received on the Sundays I was engaged in preaching. Another thing that kept our grocery bill down was the daily lunch provided to all the students by the college. Beside all this, the amazing child allowance was very welcome income.

The issue of personal poverty had arisen already in Glasgow, but my diary reveals that it was on my mind on the day Roger was born, 30th November 1963, (another mouth to feed, I supposed!):

Diary Entry: November 1963

"Coming home from hospital, the thought came into my head, was I prepared to face poverty?" I don't think a positive answer could be given. Yet, it may be that we shall have to prepare for it. Our resources are restricted, and we may well have to do without. This should be willingly accepted though, after all, so many missionaries and other folk have too little. We have so much in some ways, perhaps, extravagance has been one of our sins!)" Here is guilt rearing its ugly head again!!

Once it was determined that I should prepare to sit for a London, Bachelor of Divinity Degree, I once again sought another grant. The County Council's amazingly generous spirit resulted in a full grant being awarded for the next three years! Certainly, financial pressures had been lifted, and once again, we were sure God was behind it. (Well, it sounds quite miraculous—which other persons in history, starting with not even one 'O' level, received financial support for five years, five whole college/university years? How much I owe the Derbyshire County Council! To this day, I am full of amazement and profound gratitude.)

About this time, we went on a search for more adequate accommodation and were over the moon when we found 64 Lancaster Avenue. We were to share a house with a widow, Mrs Gordon. She was to live downstairs and we upstairs. The only thing we shared was a bathroom. She was a gentle, kindly soul who befriended Margaret. Because the original rent quoted was too high for us, Mrs Gordon agreed a reduction 'for such nice people.'

One lovely, and yet, as it turned out, poignant happening was the unexpected visit of dad and mother. On the day they arrived, I had gone to college as usual but was called out of class; Margaret had telephoned to tell me they had called on their way to Ascot. A lovely memory still vividly with me is dad walking towards me as I walked from the bus stop with the two boys with some large blown-up balloons. Typical dad! He was such a fun person! One regret is that after he told me he was ill and didn't expect to live long, I inadequately responded, "Oh I'm sure you'll be all right." Dad was, therefore, denied an opportunity to say what was on his mind. This was the last time I was to see him, and my immaturity prevented a serious conversation.

At the age of forty-six, dad died in the hospital when his pancreas burst. My mother was in the house belonging to the pub dad worked in. Also in the house was my seventeen-year-old brother, Trevor. For quite some time, mother and Trevor were allowed to run the pub. Fortunately, dad had a premonition he would die young, so he had taken out life insurance. Mother then was able to buy a home.

Generous Trevor Martin, another student, drove me and the family to mother's for the funeral. We lodged with Margaret's family until the actual day. The funeral itself, together with the huge reception in Pilsley Miners' Welfare, left a deep impression on me. By the end of the day, it sadly dawned on me that I'd never really known dad, and certainly hadn't appreciated him. To see the congregation in church was the first shock. Yes, dad came from a large family, and he was steward of one of Warsop's pubs, but the church was absolutely packed. People at dad's funeral reception, family members and friends spoke of his generosity. Apparently, at the hospital, shortly after mother had been told about the results of the necessary autopsy, she met the local Warsop policeman who expressed his condolences. "They've just told me that Bill had a small heart." "Oh no Nellie," the policeman retorted, "he had a big un!" The guilt in me surged, almost overwhelmingly, and in the subsequent months and even years, I allowed bitterness and resentment to eat away the best parts of myself. None of the faculty came to my rescue—I have no recollection of even one of them asking about dad, and as for the students, I suppose, like myself, they were too young and inexperienced to be of much help. Not surprisingly, I began to ask serious questions about God and religion. I had not yet understood the need to grieve. Following the English public-school tradition, I decided to keep a stiff upper lip, believing it would help support mother. The refusal to mourn and this suppression of feelings had a profound effect, so much so that it determined my emotional response to the Spurgeon's experience for the next three years. Quite deliberately, I focussed on all that was wrong with the college.

Another event that fed and watered all this negativity was my first sermon class. Every week, one student was expected to preach a prepared, and previously written-out, sermon. The faculty and other students would then, afterwards, make public comments. Two students who had received a copy of the sermon would be proffered time to make prepared criticisms. The unexpected blow, for me, was when the tutor, Frank Fitzsimmons, stood to apparently enjoy the opportunity of a character assassination. Partly, what hurt most was that some students agreed with the assessment of my character (Even at the time, I really knew the truth!). But how deeply it hurt! Immediately afterwards, my dear friend, Peter Edwards, took me to his room and commiserated. He graciously attempted to comfort and reassure me. One thing, however, stayed rooted in the mind. Sermon class had been abused; it was intended to criticise a sermon not a person! Off, I went to see the principal. He suggested a meeting take place between the two combatants in the presence of two student officers, David Coffee and Peter Judd, two members of my own batch. The meeting did not go well! I became too emotional whilst Fitzsimmons was able to remain cool, calm and collected. (He was as cool as a cucumber—stiff and starchy.) Although we shook hands, there had certainly been no reconciliation. It was to prove to be an encounter never to be forgotten—importantly, the feelings of humiliation and deep hurtfulness remained. What a pity, there was no one who could interpret what was happening, so they might intervene to prevent a destructive festering.

One can see in hindsight how my emotional negativity began to undermine my beliefs. Yes, I resented what God had allowed—but was there really a God, up there, to be angry with? It transpired that there were several periods when serious doubts took over. The occasion, for example, when I trotted into Peter's room to blurt out, "I don't think that I believe in it anymore." Dear Peter's reaction was "but John, you're one of the best preachers I've ever heard." I retorted it was possible to preach when one's convictions were firm, but at that time, I was all at sea. Interestingly, Peter said that he never had doubts. No, for all the time I knew him, up to his untimely death, he was consistent—both in his convictions and in his practice as a Christian man.

My determination, most of the time, was to fight for the recovery of my faith. Periods of doubt didn't disappear. In one of these periods, sharing the dilemma with Margaret, I raised the idea of going into teaching—for the time had arrived, when even atheists were appointed to teach religious education in schools. So, I plodded on—becoming more cynical and bitter but working hard in what, hopefully, was not a forlorn ambition to earn a degree.

On the practical side, each of us was required to help in the extensive garden; there were fixed hours each term. The students themselves appointed officers to deal with various necessary activities. It was a delight to have the pleasant task of handing out some of the Sunday's preaching money, following my appointment as deputy treasurer! Despite all protestations to the contrary, I've always enjoyed money!

The last three years seemed to merge into one long haul. I couldn't wait for release! Was this in any way related to my ceasing, for the whole of that time, to keep a diary? (The last entry, in fact, was 29th December 1964!) Was it that confusion, disappointment, even disillusion prevailed and left me feeling unenthusiastic, empty, unsure, insincere?

Unsurprisingly, there were some much happier episodes. Family holidays were very enjoyable. Every year, provision was made for a good week's family holiday. One holiday, in the summer of 1966, was spent in a Bournemouth Christian Guest House. The lovely, warm-hearted landlady babysat one night so that Margaret and I could visit a cinema for a screening of 'The Sound of Music.'

Just prior to that, I had been sent to take services in Ventnor Baptist Church, in the Isle of Wight (Whilst there, I met a bedridden man who was over one hundred years old. He had heard the incomparable Charles Haddon Spurgeon. It seemed such a privilege to meet him and offer prayers.). A lovely couple, who had retired from London, provided the weekend hospitality in their very modest but much-loved, part-cottage. The cottage was in St Lawrence. On the bus journey from Ryde to Ventnor, the landscape had taken my breath away. Naturally, I sat on the upper deck to get the best view. The coast in St Lawrence was spectacularly beautiful, and Ventnor sported an excellent sandy beach. When told about a cottage in St Lawrence that was being used as a fully furnished holiday let, I, as soon as possible, booked it for the following year, where we could spend a fortnight between my leaving college and being inducted at my first church.

Reverting to the Bournemouth holiday a few weeks later, I was able to point children across the sea to the Needles on the Isle of Wight to explain that was where we would take a holiday the following year.

A short holiday was taken in the easter break in a Hastings Guest House, only a few weeks before the university exams. It seemed a sensible thing to do, take a short break from exhaustive study. It was in Hastings that we bought what I think was our very first picture; this reflected an appreciation of countryside—the painter was David

Shepard and the picture's title was 'March Sun.' I was to gaze and gaze at it over the years, so much so, that decades later it is possible to accurately picture it in my mind's eye. The painting cost all of ten shillings!

The landlords were warm, generous people, but there were embarrassing moments due to there being only one toilet for quite a large group of guests, and, like many men, I often took a long time on the toilet!

Some months before the end of the final year, leaving students were interviewed by George Beasley-Murray about where their first postings may be. The principal was taken aback on learning that I had decided on a comparatively small area for where my ministry should be— Derbyshire/South Yorkshire. Despite the paucity of Baptist Churches, one opportunity did arise. Wheatley Park, Doncaster, invited me to visit to 'preach with a view.' Margaret accompanied me. Mr & Mrs Williams met us at Doncaster railway station and provided generous hospitality. They were a couple in their late sixties, quite traditional; Mrs Williams ran the 'Sisterhood,' where each week a group of thirty or so older women gathered for a service of hymns, prayers and an address given by the minister, his wife, or a visiting speaker.

I met the Deacons, lay-leaders of the church. When one of them asked how I responded to criticism, I fumbled, knowing that criticism was not something I was capable of dealing with in a mature manner. At least if only part consciously, I realised rather than criticism, my deep need was for encouragement, if not fulsome praise, on account of a nagging insecurity, which though I couldn't then articulate it, held me in its thrall. In all the time spent in the ministry, that's for the next thirteen years, my need for others to affirm me, by expressions of appreciation, was a major cause of turmoil both in my emotions and in relationships with family, friends, as well as 'enemies.' The use of that last word is deliberate for those who were not 'for us' must be 'against us!'

Looking back, many years later, it was possible to see that the insecurity arose from lack of confidence in one's abilities, tensions in marriage, struggles with 'beliefs' and a part-realisation that I wasn't really good with people, unless they happened to be 'on my side!'

Having met the Deacons, chatted with members of the congregation and taken the two Sunday services, the congregation had at least been given some idea as to who and what I was. The very young church secretary, John Sanderson, who had only recently transferred his allegiance from the Methodist Church, was extremely enthusiastic about the prospect of me taking on the challenge. With a membership of around sixty, though even some of those members were inactive, the congregation, especially on Sunday morning, was rather thin.

The church was a modern building with a 'shack' (the original church), now being used as a church hall for groups like the Girls Brigade. For years, financial aid had come from 'The Home Mission Fund,' monies provided by the national 'Baptist Union,' for 'mission' churches. Many such churches never became financially independent, but the financial support provided from national resources enabled such congregations to employ a full-time minister. Understandably, the salary or stipend, as it is named, was modest; in 1967, it was £700.00. At Wheatley Park, ten shillings a week was provided as expenses to cover such things as bus fares and any other out-of-pocket expenses.

Soon after returning to London, a formal invitation arrived, which I promptly accepted. Another visit soon took place over an easter weekend. The gates were now open to begin an unknown journey in the ministry. Six years of training had been completed, but the amazing reality is that I was quite unprepared for any 'pastoral-caring' work, and the challenge of leading a weekly Bible study, as well as preparing and preaching two sermons a week. (My collection of sermons was minimal; I had been content to visit churches from Spurgeon's and use the same handful of sermons.)

But now, back to college. For several months, study was regarded as all-important. Margaret must sometimes have felt desperate!

Exam dates, all eight of them, were set for early June 1967. It was necessary to travel to London. The set papers were NT Greek, New

Testament, Old Testament, Philosophy of Religion, Ancient Church History, Modern Church History and, what I so loved, 'Historical Theology.'

The great relief of seeing my results displayed on a board outside the university cannot be exaggerated; there it was on the 'pass list:'

JOHN MELVIN HAYES

The lad who left school at fifteen had now, aged twenty-seven, achieved a Bachelor of Divinity Degree. A Graduate of London University! It hurt that my dad wasn't there to share the joy.

Obtaining this degree gave me some kudos. On arrival at Wheatley Park, I discovered there were three other Baptist Ministers in the town, and none of whom sported a degree.

Graduation day at Spurgeon's arrived, none too soon for me. Like all the other leavers, I was asked to quote a preferred verse of scripture. My choice was from St Paul 'Presenting everyone mature in Christ.' Wow! I was aiming impossibly high!

Preparations were now in hand for the move north, but first, a holiday. The train was taken to Portsmouth Harbour, then the ferry to Ryde Pier. Former London underground stock took us from there into the town where we caught a bus for the last leg of the journey. What a fabulous holiday it turned out to be! We were directed to Steephill Cove, an idyllic spot that was perfect for playing in lovely sand, paddling in what was a fairly safe sea and pottering about in the rock pools. All four of us fell in love with it all. (In subsequent years, we all noticed, particularly, how 'tense' Andrew completely relaxed in the place.)

John M Hayes

Chapter Five
FOLLOWING A VOCATION DONCASTER AND CHESHAM – FOURTEEN YEARS

By the time we moved into 2a Monmouth Drive, the Doncaster Manse, my faith seemed strong again. Margaret appeared to be happy too. At that time, she also looked her best. For the Ordination and Induction services, she wore a beautiful outfit—even a miniskirt, which suited her perfectly. Some of my family were present at the services. A joy of mine was to see Grandad Ben, one of those whom I most respected and liked. It was generous of my relations to participate, especially as not one of them professed any religious faith. Sadly, my dad, who would have been delighted to be present, was, of course, absent; this hurt me as I know how much it would have meant to him. Years later, Trevor, my brother, said, "Dad thought the world of you."

From this time, I began to keep a diary consistently. Somehow, I had managed to suppress previous doubts, and there are many positive entries. The Ordination and the Induction services, held on the same day, were full of joy. Some of the people who had influenced me in earlier years took part: John Grainger, Norman Roberts, laymen, one from Hasland, and the other New Whittington. The ministers and preachers, David Neil, who preached at our wedding, and the Venerable Rev George Young of Glasgow also took part. To have these links with the past, gave one a great sense of continuity.

The church, a new building, with an original one now used as the church hall, was situated on the edge of a huge council estate.

Just over the road was an extensive private development; most of the congregation came from there or from other areas of the town. It is simply a historical fact that churches have rarely made any inroads into the working classes.

My activity soon became routine. Mornings were spent in the study (I loved this space.), reading and preparing two sermons for Sunday, and a Bible study for the mid-week meeting. Preaching was given priority in a typical Baptist Church, so I spent about eight hours on each sermon. Afternoons were taken up with visiting some of the older people. Bible study and prayer meeting took up one evening each week, then there were monthly Deacons' meetings and irregular church meetings. Gradually, I became involved with other Chrisitan groups in the town, sometimes attending a day-time event, more often, an evening meeting. A supportive group of Baptist Ministers from the South Yorkshire area met once a month, taking it in turns to gather in the mornings in their homes. (About ten usually attended these ministerial gatherings.) Monthly morning meetings were also established for the four of us who were based in Doncaster. Besides all this, a funeral would turn up from time to time.

I quickly made friends with the Vicar of St Mary's, Wheatley, and, especially, his Curate Marc, who lived within a few yards of our Manse. Marc and his wife were of similar age to us, and they also had young children. As time went by, the three of us worked together in one way or another—I became less sectarian and more ecumenical in outlook. Nevertheless, my evangelistic passion remained very much alive. I was determined to 'save souls!' My desire for a deep spiritual life remained. Almost one hour every day, in the study, would find me on my knees in prayer. My relation to God, far from being cerebral, was intensely personal and emotional. It is significant that my first letter to the church members, written six months before the Induction services, urges people, above all else, to pray, in particular at the weekly group prayer meeting.

One of the loveliest aspects of being in Wheatley Park was that my dear friend Peter Edwards and another college friend Boyd Williams lived in Yorkshire. Peter had a church in Hull and Boyd one in York. For nearly seven years, we spent a day together with our families, about once a quarter. These were encounters to look forward to! (They were resumed some years later, when I was based in Chesham, Peter in Wickham and, finally, Boyd in Southwell, on his return from Brazil.)

Days off were important. Walking, especially in Derbyshire, was so rewarding. For once, I could relax and escape the pressure of being a church leader.

Diary entry: 4th September

"Around Kinder Scout. Gale force winds. Had to turn back at Kinder Downfall. Very exciting." (This entry doesn't even begin to do justice to the experience.)

First of all, it is significant that on one of the very first 'days off,' I chose Kinder Scout. Of course, the place is legendary with ramblers, so it was something I so much wanted to do. To climb it on such a wet, windy day, however, was foolhardy—it could easily have ended in disaster. During the whole time scrambling up Grindsbrooke, then walking on the Rim to the waterfall and back, not one other soul was encountered. Only when I reached the bottom track back to Edale, did I meet a couple from London, who were on holiday. What an experience though, and one repeated only a few times in the rest of my life. (The final climb was taken in September 2019, when I was seventy-nine. For several years, it had been a personal ambition to scramble up just one more time. A young friend agreed to accompany me, with his first aid box! David Hunter had climbed Kinder with me before, but then, we took the easier, but more boring route from Hayfield, the route the famous Trespassing Ramblers took in the 1930s. This time we took the original Pennine Way route.)

For the next seven years, on my Thursday days off, most days would see me somewhere in the Peak District, travelling there by train and bus via Sheffield. Later, on discovering Clumber Park, I sometimes walked there for a change. Both locations came to have a special place in my life—and to this day, they still do. It was the

Curate Marc Seccombe who introduced me to Clumber very early on in our time in Doncaster. One day, he crammed his family and mine into his small Citroen car; we felt like sardines in a tin! But what a lovely visit it turned out to be.

Quite early on, it came as a shock how small the church congregations were, especially so on Sunday mornings. In fact, only sixty names appeared on the membership roll, and it transpired even some of these had lapsed. To some extent, I would now say, in an unhealthy way, I became obsessed with numbers, even counting the people as a service progressed. One of the underlying motives was a desire to be successful, although this was only something I was prepared to acknowledge much later in life. But there was also a genuine concern 'to bring more people to Christ.' In 1968, before one whole year of ministry had been completed, I took up an idea that did result in reaching more people, as well as transforming some evening services. At this time, a number of churches had established lively singing groups, mainly young people, with musicians and guitarists, in an effort to reach out to youngsters who were outside the church and who would not be attracted by a traditional church service. On the first trial, my sister-in-law Joyce and her husband Keith came over from Chesterfield with 'The Jubilees.' After contributing to the service, we moved over to the dilapidated hall, where a coffee bar had been set up. It amazed us how many people attended, and some of the Boys Brigade were present. The event was judged to be a success so more were planned.

At this time, following the premature death of Arthur Knight, the treasurer, a financial crisis emerged. A younger man, Albert Stephenson, volunteered to act as treasurer, and his efforts eventually transformed the finances. His stance was simply that members should be told how much was required and contribute accordingly.

I think, sadly, it reflects badly on me that there is no diary entry for my daughter Rachel's birth. This is yet another example of my obsession with religion, to the extent that such an important family event was overlooked. (In fact, there was no mention of Rachel's birth anywhere in the diary!) Let me make amends now!

Rachel Margaret was born in hospital on 19th February 1968, just one day after my birthday! Now, we were a family of five. Rachel was utterly adorable; the church folk took to her. Amazingly, she seemed, even at such a tender age, sociable and engaging with one and all. For so many years, this was Rachel. Over the dinner table, when she was about four, I blurted out "we all love mummy don't we;" this then went round the table in turn, first to me, then Andrew, then Roger until we reached Rachel. Following the turn "we all love Rachel don't we," Rachel left me gobsmacked by uttering "I love everybody; I even love myself!" Subsequently, I often quoted it, most pointedly when preaching on the text 'Love Your Neighbour as Yourself;' I also mentioned it in a speech at her wedding. She had unconsciously grasped what many even adults never do—it is essential if one is to have a good life, that one has respect for oneself.

As 1968 went on, a few more people became members of the congregation, some merely transferring membership from another church in the town; such were Gordon and Ruth Bennett, who were to have a profound impact not only on the church but also on me personally. The congregation was gradually increasing in size. Some new members had moved to Doncaster with their job, including a doctor and several teachers. Apparently, it was largely my preaching that attracted them. These newcomers changed the complexion of the congregation. All the newcomers were young couples, who were of an evangelical persuasion; they professed a very deep commitment to Christ—nothing vague here! One or two of these new folk were excellent pianists who eventually took over from Mr Pike the regular, faithful organist. Their style of playing was different and, eventually, a rota of them enlivened and enriched the services. At the end of my first year of service, we set off for that holiday, long reserved and anticipated, in St Lawrence, Isle of Wight. Being without a car, we travelled by train. My sister had, sometime previously, bought our two boys a premium bond each; Roger's came up with a £50.00 win.

With part of the proceeds, we enjoyed breakfast in the dining car. I can well remember the kindness of the chief steward who took a lively interest in the children. On we went, catching a train to Portsmouth Harbour. Then, onto a ferry, a new experience for the children. For the last part of the journey, we went by bus, passing through the wonderful landscape, which had enthralled me previously. Finally, we walked from the bus stop to Rowan Cottage. This was a substantial and fully furnished house. On recommendations, days were spent in Steephill Cove. Each of us was very happy, and even in subsequent years, when we occupied a new flat at the end of Ventnor seafront, we would still walk over to the cove. Those were wonderful holidays when Andrew finally became less tense and seemed relaxed, which even young Rachel perceived.

Back in Doncaster, the four Wheatley ministers, Alan Shires (Vicar), Marc Seccombe (Curate), Stanley Clayton (Methodist) and myself became increasingly close. A consultation was held with a Church Army Captain on how the four churches could work together in the area.

Diary Entry: 24th February 1969

"Four Wheatley ministers met at 9.05 a.m. for payer. We are going to do this once a fortnight." (Subsequently, apart from Stanley, three of us met almost daily for a time.)

Pushing on into 1969, a lot of change was taking place, both to the congregation, as well as to the format of Sunday services.

Diary Entry: 15th March 1969

"We're living in a time of transition; old patterns are rapidly going out. The patterns of having two identical Sunday services seems to be dying out."

"I must not be either reactionary or too revolutionary."

By June 1970, everything certainly seemed to be on the march.

Diary Entry: June
"The tide had turned."

Diary Entry: 29th September
"Record attendance for Harvest Festival yesterday—morning service 40 and evening service 125+. The Worship Group's first big effort was a success—even older folk thought it was good."

The abovementioned worship group had been established earlier in the year. A drama teacher had recently joined the church, who, with my encouragement, formed and ran the group; it was open to anyone in the congregation. These people met with me in the Manse, where after I had informed them of the theme chosen for a particular Sunday, some drama or dance or just readings were planned around it. Eventually, news spread of what was happening, and the group were invited to perform in a few other churches.

One involvement for me, outside of the church, was participating in Alan Shires 'Clinical Theology' sessions at the Vicarage. A handful of clergy and ministers joined. Alongside this, an awareness of the growing influence of Pentecostalism caused me to read, think and talk more about that. In their very different ways, both were to have a profound impact on my personal life and ministry in Doncaster, including an involvement with psychiatric patients, and an immersive personal counselling service.

The idea of Clinical Theology was to bring the insights of psychology into mainstream Christian pastoral care. For some time, going back to my college days, a sense that some knowledge of the subject may be helpful in pastoral care had resided at the back of my mind. Participating in Alan's sessions, opened my eyes to some of the psychological problems people had, including my own! Some of the new understanding also challenged the judgemental tendency traditionally adopted by the church. Within two years of my Ordination, I was beginning to see a lot of things differently.

Diary Entry: 22nd July 1969

"Read Lee's book 'Your Growing Child and Religion.' He talks a lot of sense. Must read through again. Becoming increasingly interested in psychology. Yet, I know one must be careful not to let psychotherapy become a substitute for preaching the Gospel. However, I'm beginning to see that folk in my congregation could probably be helped to live more adequately through the help of psychotherapy, or something like it.

Actually, I'm not sure what I'm on about."

The last sentence reveals my sense of confusion. Certainly, the new knowledge was causing me to re-examine some ideas, but as yet, I'd only just put my toe into the water.

One of the members of St Mary's was a Dr Alan Wilson, a psychiatrist at the Doncaster Royal Infirmary. We became friends and co-workers. Dr Wilson came to see me on 7th October 1970. He felt an inadequacy in helping his patients. As a firm believer, he was convinced that God was the one who could meet people's deep needs. He wanted me to become involved with one of his patients, a stunning looking young woman who had ended up in hospital after slitting her wrists. (This woman, with two children, did recover her equanimity.) Later, I was invited to engage with the drug clinic that Dr Wilson voluntarily ran once a week. There were something like thirty to forty individuals who depended on this clinic.

Diary Entry: 12th February 1971

"Yesterday made my first contact with the drug addicts at Dr Wilson's clinic. I spent four exhausting hours. The idea is that once a fortnight I should mingle and talk with the addicts in the waiting hall.

There is a possibility of my being appointed Free Church Chaplain in the Psychiatric Block."

Soon after this date, I was so appointed. The position also included responsibilities at Loversall, a small psychiatric hospital in the town.

These appointments were welcome and turned out to be deeply satisfying. My awakened interest in 'what made people tick,' and how they may be supported, if not healed, now took a steep learning curve. One often felt inadequate, if not quite useless, so it was amazing and encouraging, some years after the position had been relinquished, to hear my successor say that some of the Loversall staff told him that I brought peace onto the wards! Just the sort of encouragement for which I was always so hungry!

I got to know several of the addicts, even visiting them in their homes. More than one funeral was held for one of them who had accidently overdosed. At Dr Wilson's request, I drove one couple to Mapperley in Nottingham to a drugs rehabilitation centre. Bill and Ann Dancy were heroin addicts, I'd befriended; she was one of the most beautiful young women one could find. (A few years later, down the grapevine, it was reported they were free from drugs. Apparently, the motivation to rehabilitate was Ann's desire to have a baby. Until then, nothing else worked.)

Diary Entry: 28th April 1971

"Peter Z came for a chat tonight. He has a psychological difficulty, and hopes next month to see Dr Wilson.

I am becoming more and more involved in psychology and psychological disturbances. I wonder if there is a diploma in psychiatry one can take?

The Clinical Theology Group continues to be stimulating. We had a session this morning."

My friendship with Dr Wilson developed. One day, he even came to share a domestic problem and to seek my help! He was such a humble person who, as I told him more than once, underestimated his own ability and worth. On the evening that he came to seek my advice, he stayed until 11.15 p.m.

Parallel to all this stimulating work, I began to take an interest in Pentecostalism. Ruth Bennett, who had belonged to the Doncaster Pentecostal Church for most of her life, had more recently been drawn to the modern Pentecostal or 'Charismatic Movement,' which had arisen and was spreading in mainstream churches. A group called 'The Fountain Trust' had been formed and was leading a campaign to encourage the movement. An Anglican priest and his wife, Michael and Jan Harper, worked full time for the trust. One evening, Gordon and Ruth Bennett hosted a small group meeting in their home, where together with several other Doncaster church ministers, I met the couple. I was, at this point, interested but very cautious, as per a diary entry record.

Diary Entry: 22nd April 1971

"After visiting two folk s in hospital, I finally ended up at Ruth Bennett's. She had disturbed me just a little. I'm afraid her Pentecostal views may be leading her astray somewhat. She and Gordon have been very gracious to me and others, who have not had their experiences. I only hope now that she does not make too much of these experiences."

On the other hand, I hope to remain very open to receive guidance about such things as a healing ministry and the exercise of spiritual gifts.

It has done me good writing this down. Now to the sermons!"

By early 1971, I was being drawn in, as by a magnet; I even attended a residential Fountain Trust Conference.

Diary Entry: 6th May 1971

"I have just returned from attending my first Fountain Trust Conference at High Leigh. It was stimulating and useful. I have been given much food for thought. In fact, I've got beyond the thinking stage—one must begin to act!"

It is fascinating that through these two influences, psychology and the Charismatic Movement, my ministry was, gradually, moving in a direction very different to that of the traditional Baptist minister!

Throughout this time, my tense inner self persisted, as usual. I was still getting relief on Thursdays from country walks.

John M Hayes

Diary Entry: July 1971

"*Thursday long-standing ambition to walk over the ridge surrounding Castleton. Began at Hathersage, climbed Wyn Hill, ended at the 'shivering mountain.' Walked seventeen miles.*"

Another day, I headed for Lathkill Dale. After enjoying it so much, I somehow managed to return with all the family. We must have been amazingly fit. Of course, even both Margaret and I were still in our twenties! In my mind now, I can see Roger, not yet six, thoroughly enjoying being allowed to splash through the water overflowing onto the path; no doubt, he couldn't believe his luck.

One day, Alan Elland, a fellow student at the BTI, turned up in Wheatley. He was a Methodist who had become a missionary with the OMF. We went walking together on a day when we were both free.

Diary Entry: 26th January 1971

"*Yesterday took Alan Elland walking in Derbyshire... The trip to Baslow, Froggatt Edge and Grindleford was magnificent. The weather was exceptional—Spring anticipated.*"

Once we got a car, Clumber Park became a regular destination. Many times, I would pack a picnic, then meet the children who were all in schools on our doorstep, then drive to pick up Margaret, whose latest post was at Intake School, again quite nearby, and head for Clumber Park. These were marvellous times, which were sadly cut short when I had to return for an evening meeting, for example, like a Deacons meeting. (Clumber featured greatly in my new life, many years later.)

Margaret had returned to teaching, which she loved. The Director of Education, who was a member of our church, found her a job, when Rachel was only about three years old. The school was some distance away, but later, Margaret managed to find a post almost within walking distance of our house.

Another favourite haunt was Padley Gorge. On one occasion, when we were staying at Margaret's parents' place, we drove out to the Gorge.

Diary Entry: 2nd June 1972

"Mainly because of bad weather, our plans for walking were thwarted. However, we spent some time outside each day. For the first time, I identified a linnet (near Crich) and a wood warbler (Padley Gorge)."

Although it was wonderful that the whole family could relish being in the countryside, I still felt it necessary to have walking days on my own.

Although on a modest income, in the first year or so, in Doncaster, we made saving up for a fortnight's holiday in the Isle of Wight a priority. As already recorded, the early journeys were by train. Once a car was available, we had more flexibility, but the Isle of Wight continued to be our chosen destination.

Diary Entry: 11th September 1970

"Just home from a fabulous holiday in the Isle of Wight. Lasting about three weeks, it was the longest we've ever had. Four days we spent in Yarmouth. The car performed well. I've come home though to a bill for £43.00 from Roodhouses Garage.

In spite of all Margaret has earned, we remain in debt. Wherever does all the cash go?

Besides the open countryside, I thoroughly enjoy our own small garden. With Mr Staton's help, I even managed to grow some vegetables." (Margaret's father was an experienced and avid gardener.)

Diary Entry: 28th August 1970

"I've been tidying the garden—it is beginning to look very nice. The lawn at the front is looking well. What we need now is a few interesting plants for the rockery. The path around my study also needs attention. Deacons have said I can buy a fence—this will make a big difference. At the moment, the field grows into my garden."

Diary Entry: Easter Day 1971

"... and the sun is quickly melting a heavy frost, what a glorious beginning to the day. The birds dawn chorus began at 5 a.m. I was up at 6.15 a.m. for the service."

John M Hayes

For several years, I had delighted in observing a couple of nesting Greenfinches in a rose bush immediately outside the study window. My interest in birds continued throughout the years, and it was always a joy for me to record the observation of a new bird in the Observer's Book of British Birds.

All throughout these first four years or so, lots of books were read, besides my religious ones. My diary contains several references to what was being read. This reading was certainly increasing my knowledge—the books were certainly 'food for thought.' A few diary extracts support this memory.

Diary Entry: 30th June 1968
"Read some of Glorious Company—useful for children."
We were now about five years into the ministry at Wheatley Park, but this entry shows that my inner turmoil had, in no way, subsided.

Diary Entry: 20th April 1972
"Five months since my last entry. How time flies! I have again been reluctant to write because of personal struggles and failures."

It does appear, reading these repeated 'depressing' entries, that psychologically my state was unhealthy, and if nothing positive and helpful happened soon, I would have been a casualty, with a nasty 'breakdown.

Our marriage was a contributory factor, especially my personal inadequacy as a husband and father. Margaret was a shy person, but I was dominant. In some respects, I wished that Margaret would have been more lively, more of an equal. Our sex life was alive, probably, more so than many couples, but I wasn't content and wished it could be more lively! The fundamental problem though was not sexual but emotional. There was a lack of true intimacy. On my side, it had always been difficult to show emotion, just like my dad and mother, I suppose. Later, even with my children, showing warmth and tenderness didn't come naturally. One would have thought that as Margaret and I shared a faith that we were both sincerely devoted to, this may have brought us closer. The reality was that we were quite incapable of talking about spirituality at a personal level. There were times of joy, but the underlying emotion, on my part at least, was of disappointment, even if one couldn't put one's finger on it. Deeply sad it was! Yet, there were obviously periods when the clouds lifted, so one must be careful of exaggeration.

Diary Entry: 26th June 1971

"Margaret and I are experiencing great happiness together. I suppose it has helped having the financial burden lifted from us. What is there on Earth to compare with true love and a happy relationship in marriage? Lately, several marital problems have come my way, and in dealing with the people concerned, it has been a help to have, myself, a more stable relationship."

When I recently read these words, I was shocked. Obviously, I've remembered more of the bad times!

Diary Entry: 6th December 1971

"Margaret is very settled. I just wonder sometimes how much time she gives to cultivating the things of the spirit. It is difficult to tell. We have never found it easy to discuss personal, spiritual matters, either together, or with anyone else. Maybe, it is a matter of our personality and makeup.

…A lot of my trouble though is being out of touch with God, which leads to embarrassment at talking about him." (In this passage, apart from anything else, my judgemental attitude towards my wife is explicit. Margaret had to put up with a judgemental husband. No doubt, his own 'failure' was projected onto her.)

One of the biggest strains on the marriage, and one that persisted for many years, was coping with our emotionally difficult first child: Andrew.

Diary Entry: 16th November 1970

"Andrew's birthday today. He was happy to receive cards and gifts. Such a sensitive boy; I ought to be more careful how I treat him. I shout too much."

These words suggest a feeling of inadequacy. At that time, it would have been impossible to show tenderness by giving a hug, for example.

Diary Entry: 27th January 1971

"For months, Andrew has been 'impossible.' Margaret and I have been worried and at a loss as to what to do. Just now, as I was praying, an idea I'd conceived, long ago, came into sharper focus. A great deal of my difficulty in handling the situation stems from a hurt pride. What upsets me so much is that my boy should be so uncooperative, stubborn, unkind and selfish. Perhaps, if I swallowed my pride, my own vicious temper would subside."

Extracts in my diary vividly reveal my state of mind at the time.

It would no doubt seem extreme to an outsider, but to this day, the conflict and resulting agony have never been forgotten. Although there were many happier emotions, the destructive ones were always under the surface. I felt guilt, failure and, at times, almost despair.

Of course, the prayers for help were not answered. Sometimes, this disappointment made me wonder if God really existed!

More diary entries reveal the problems persisted.

Diary Entry: 21st July 1971

"For a few weeks, I've been in the pit of despair. Prayer has almost totally disappeared. At times, I wondered what would happen. All sorts of silly ideas entered my head, like going into teaching. How I've carried on I don't know, feeling so weak, guilty and unprepared for ministry. I'm hardly in a fit state to lead a congregation, or even my own family, for that matter.

Nevertheless, we plod on."

My overly serious nature was never interested in 'superficial pleasures.' All the fun most people enjoyed at Christmas evaded me; I simply couldn't let myself go and join in the festivities (apart from eating).

Diary Entry: Christmas Eve 1971

"I always have periods of depression at Christmas. My failure is, practically, to enjoy all the good things in life."

Clearly, even then I had some self-awareness. I was taking life too seriously, not accepting that life should include fun, happiness and enjoying family life!

Diary Entry:

"Periods of depression come and go. I wonder if my depressions are more serious than what is experienced by the average man. What causes them when I'm in normal health?

Not enough work?

Disappointment at progress in myself or in the church?

Laziness?

Sin, especially a besetting one?

Failure in meditation and prayer?

I soon get 'fed-up' looking after the children or pottering about with jobs in the house."

Looking back decades later, it seems to me that I had unrealistic aspirations and a distorted view of things.

The success of my church, certainly, had something to do with my self-esteem, my craving for recognition, and my need to be affirmed. Well, I certainly got all of this. (There were, I'm sure a few people who saw through me; they discerned my passion for God was not all altruistic, but there were underlying psychological needs, demanding to be fed.) 'Wanting to be different'—yes, there it was again!

Up to the Spring of 1972, the church growth was, almost, exponential. Since its inception in 1941, Wheatley Part Baptist Church had been heavily dependent on the 'Home Mission Fund.' Regular payments had been received right up to my Induction in 1967. As the membership and congregation grew, and the treasurer's stewardship improved, the point was reached in 1971, when this dependency could become a thing of the past. A special service with the area's Senior Minister Reverend Hugh Reid was held to mark the very significant transition.

Underneath all the seriousness, and at times depression, I believe my real nature contained more joy. This aspect of me blossomed once I'd left the church and abandoned religion. Many years later, a Mr Biggin, whose restaurant in Riber I frequented, invited me and Maggie to lunch. When he asked if I knew why he'd invited me, I felt embarrassed, after all I could hardly say "because I am one of your best customers." Fortunately, before there was time to respond Mr Biggin came to the rescue. "It's because of your joie de vivre!" This quite threw me, but on reflection, I understood. Many years later, on my 80th birthday, Sharon, an employee in our Chesterfield office, wrote in a birthday card: "Your joy and passion have served you well." Much, much later, Angela, Maggie's daughter, wrote something similar in a birthday card. On the front was written SOME PEOPLE MISS THE LITTLE JOYS OF LIFE, WHILE WAITING FOR THE BIG ONES THAT NEVER SHOW UP. Inside Angela had written "John, whereas, you take every joy from life."

But this is running ahead of myself—back to Doncaster.

Chapter Six
ANOTHER WATERSHED – JUNE 1972 A LIBERATING, LIFE-ENHANCING EXPERIENCE

At the age of thirty-two, five years into the Doncaster ministry, a remarkable experience occurred that gave me much more hope, both with my personal struggles and the related matter, our marriage.

Through Ruth Bennett, I became aware of an American 'leader,' Anne White. She led a ministry with a name that I'm surprised didn't put me off: 'Victorious Ministry Through Christ (VMTC).' In June 1972, I travelled with Ruth Bennett to a Diocesan Retreat Centre for a week of prayer counselling. During the conference, every person was enabled to have a personal session. Mine came half-way through the week. Two Anglican lay people took my session, the male church warden of a famous church in Bristol, known as 'Pip & Js,' and 'Mary,' a member of an equally famous church in Kensington, London. From the talks and 'testimony' of those who had already received counselling, I had some inkling of what to expect. My session lasted for several hours. One of the beneficial aspects of this form of counselling was that there was no time limit to it. What transpired in those hours was transformative! At one point, I was asked to explain why I'd grown a beard, which led to the memory of my mother saying, "Our John should have been a girl." All at once the illumination came, I had never fully felt my masculinity! During the session, it came into my mind that whenever a church service was being shared with Alan Shires and Stanley Clayton, two tall and robed ministers, 'little' John, in his ordinary suit, felt somewhat uncomfortable! Of course, what became clear was that the struggle I was having resisting girlie magazines was related to this root problem. Amazingly, this experience really did profoundly change me, and for a time, it was transformative for my marriage and for the ministry in the church. From the Diocesan Centre, I spoke to Margaret on the telephone; she told me she could tell by the sound of my voice that something profound had happened. Another issue that was resolved was the bitterness and resentment I'd harboured over my dad's premature death. These emotions had been so destructive. I was also able, once and for all, to abandon the destructive, festering resentment I'd harboured for Frank Fitzsimmons, the tutor at Spurgeon's College who had upset me. The bitterness left me to such an extent that some years later in the Chesham Church Manse I provided hospitality when he was to take Sunday's services. It was such a relief to let go of all the negative thoughts that for years scarred my life.

On returning home, a houseful of people was awaiting me; they were a motley crew of people preparing for baptism and church membership. From that moment, life became hectic. My retreat experience had released something in me; Margaret said, "You've discovered what love is!" It certainly felt like it to me. The Deacons subsequently authorised Ruth Bennett to work with me at a pastoral level. I say to work with me, but it was much more like me working with her, for she had more understanding and insight at this early stage. To my complete amazement, people in the congregation approached me for help. For months on end, Ruth and I were kept incredibly busy, so much so, I asked Margaret if she would resign from her teaching job so that she could give more support. (Here I was again, encouraging, sadly, almost demanding Margaret to sacrifice herself for me—although at the time, of course, it was for God!) The financial implications for our family were immense, but such was the tsunami of religious zeal, all sensible considerations were swept away.

For two years, nothing could hold us back. The church grew exponentially! Because of the demands, I resigned from the hospital chaplainry—such was my dedication to the new enlarged opportunity in the church. One Sunday morning, at a baptism, the congregation packed the building, even spilling out into the porch. It was funny that the Doncaster Gazette reported on it with the headline: "Church bursting at the seams." Beside the report was a photograph of girls in bathing costumes, bursting out at the seams! Dr Alan Wilson was enthusiastic about developing a healing ministry in the area. A conference on healing, which was led by myself, proved to be very popular; 'Mary,' who had counselled me at the retreat, gave me a book on healing by the Rev George Bennett, an Anglican Priest. After reading it, I noted "I would love to meet this man." Well, before long, George came to lead an Ecumenical weekend with our Anglican and Methodist friends. (I now felt perfectly comfortable standing beside Alan and Stanley.)

Throughout this wonderful time, the joy and passion that many, over the years, have associated with me were pronounced. It was a very happy time when it appeared that a lot of the tension and depression that had so often dragged me down were in retreat.

What gave me the most joy and the greatest fulfilment was the ministry of counselling. This form of counselling involved two people working with the 'patient,' usually and ideally, one member of each sex. What problems did people present with? Most of all, my eyes were opened to the prevalence of sexual abuse; this came as a huge shock. Related to this, not surprisingly, were relationship difficulties of one sort or another.

The sessions involved much listening and some praying. Ruth and I did little talking. Mostly, people came for just one session, but this could, and often did, last for hours. We met, for privacy, in my study, usually in the daytime, sometimes in the evening. One such session continued into the early hours. This case was a late middle-aged man who, generally, was not well-liked. He, however, humbly opened up and told us his story. As a young man, despite being a very active member of his church, he became involved in crime to such an extent that he was given a prison sentence. His sense of guilt had never left him and, not surprisingly, influenced his present-day relationships. What a different person was revealed in this session. As he related the story, he was, at times, in tears. In subsequent days, he seemed more relaxed, less on the defensive. What a privilege it seemed to be trusted to hear stories like this; and it was amazing to sometimes observe such a difference in people once they had shared their stories with us.

One of the most moving encounters was with an elderly lady. It was arranged for her to meet one morning in my study. For two to three hours, she poured out her concerns, whilst Ruth and I just listened. At times, Mrs S was in tears; the experiences she was relating had clearly been troubling her very deeply. Finally, at the end of it all, she sighed deeply, then exclaimed, "Oh, I've been wanting to get that out of my system all my life!" She had been relating painful experiences from childhood! Through participating in the Clinical Theology Group, I had become aware, at least theoretically, of the devasting impact some childhood experiences could have, but now, through my work, evidence of this was being uncovered in many individuals' lives. As for Mrs S, it was a joy to see her smiling, relaxed face as she looked up to me from the congregation, the following Sunday.

Another person was sent to us by the psychiatrist Dr Wilson. This was a very smartly attired businesswoman whom Dr Wilson was experiencing difficulties in helping. What a horrific childhood she had endured. Quite often her parents punished her when she didn't understand she'd done anything wrong. They had sometimes even locked her in a cupboard and left her for hours whilst they went out! Of course, the child was bewildered but was left with the feeling that she must be a very bad girl to be so severely punished. No wonder, all her adult life, the effect was a lack of confidence and self-worth.

Besides my ministry in Doncaster, I was involved nationally in what were called prayer counselling schools. These were retreats like the one I had attended. Together with a group of the Church of England clergy and senior lay people, I was appointed to the board that planned and ran the schools. Wheatly Park generously released me to assist several week-long and weekend retreats. The week-long sessions were primarily for clergy or ministers of various denominations and their wives. I was appointed to be a speaker as well as a counsellor. Once again, my eyes were opened as to how many people, even senior Christian leaders were burdened with unresolved emotional, relationship and sexual problems.

What a great privilege to be engaged in such work. Undoubtedly, I received at least as much, or even more, satisfaction as in the general church ministry. I took encouragement from realizing we were dealing with real, concrete issues. The work did also force me to challenge some of Christianity's view of right and wrong. (Eventually, this new way of thinking played a part in my total rejection of 'the faith.') When the time came to leave Wheatley Park for another church, I was delighted to receive support for continuing with this wonderful ministry.

The downside of such a deep involvement with Ruth was that an emotional attachment developed. Almost inevitably, unhealthy feelings arose between us. As with Elaine, in Glasgow, we never crossed the line sexually but each of us acknowledged what was happening between us. By now, my marriage had slid back again—some of the old tensions and temptations returned. The turmoil had a negative effect on my faith in God, though I clung on.

Why did I cling on? Well, I still believed in the Christian view of marriage. In any case, a break-up simply would have been devastating for the family. I would have lost my job, my income and our home. In any case, I still had feelings for Margaret, and, on her part, she professed to still be very much in love with me. For all these reasons, I endeavoured, over many more years, to work on the relationship. But it was often difficult. Clearly, the struggles with the marriage ran in parallel with those I was having with faith. Moreover, they were inextricably linked.

One other factor that caused stress was the behaviour of our first-born Andrew. There were early signs of problems with him, which developed a few years later. He wasn't easy to deal with, and this affected Margaret and myself, as we couldn't agree on how to deal with Andrew!

In Baptist churches, ministers are appointed by the local congregation; there is no national authority involvement, although area superintendents did assist churches to find the right person for them. After seven years in Doncaster, I came to the decision that it was time to move on. This conviction only arose after a private meeting with the church treasurer. Albert had asked to see me. It transpired that he thought it may be time for the church to have a different leader who could build on my legacy. Perhaps, it was partly due to the build-up of emotions in me, but I decided that a move should be considered. Following a meeting with the area superintendent, several churches contacted me. Three of them were visited, one in Darlington, the others in Huntingdon and Harrow. A fourth church in Chesham invited me to meet them, and once they had unanimously offered me the Pastorate, I decided to accept.

All of this coincided with the time that arrangements had been made to take a one-term sabbatical, at Wheatley Park's expense. I was to spend the Michaelmas Term among the Spires in Oxford. (A small Baptist church college, Regent's Park was affiliated to Oxford University.) I had deliberately chosen this college rather than any other, because its theological stance had, traditionally, been very different to my Spurgeon's College. It was, perhaps, a subconscious urge that persuaded me to do this. Certainly, already, I resisted the pull of the extreme Evangelicals.

Another example of my selfishness was overlooking Andrew's needs. Instead of arranging for him to lodge with a church member in Chesham, so that he could start at the local grammar school at the beginning of the term, he was left stuck in Doncaster, until halfway through term. This turned out to be disastrous. Sadly, he was forced to sit an exam, before being allowed to start at Chesham High. It seems to me that he never managed to catch up with the class. In Doncaster, his final report was glowing. Apart from all else, Andrew found the move, generally, very difficult. (For many years afterwards, I blamed the bad timing of the move for Andrew's very serious problems thereafter.)

Two of our very best friends in the church were Charles and Ruth Garratt. In the summer of 1974, they very kindly, and generously, invited us to join them for a holiday-home break in Polzeath. Never having been to Cornwall, we really looked forward to visiting. The house turned out to be comfortable, and the environment was stunning.

One evening, when I'd stayed in, whilst everyone but Rachel had gone for a stroll, I sat reading poetry.

Diary Entry: 24th July 1974

"A copy of John Betjeman's 'High and Low' lies at my elbow. When I opened it and discovered that some of the poems were about Cornwall, I was delighted." One of the poems was actually about Polzeath Bay. The bay made a deep impression on me.

Diary Entry:

"At each end of the bay are two islands guarding sentinels. To watch the waves, through binoculars, as they beat against the islands is a moving sight."

Diary Entry: 26th July

"Charles has a fine pair of binoculars, and they enabled us to identify shags, terns, oystercatchers, great black-backed gulls and, less certainly, guillemots. The rock formations of the cliffs are weirdly contorted and strips of green or white rock are clearly discerned in the grey slate."

During the holiday, I enjoyed reading not only poetry but also books by Archbishop Anthony Bloom, an Orthodox Church priest.

Diary Entry: 27th July

"Charles says he finds Anthony Bloom difficult. We agreed different authors appeal to us at different periods of our life. The difference is personality, as Ruth pointed out."

Diary Entry: 4th August

"Once again, the sunset is fantastic. I enjoy sitting at this writing desk and glancing out of the window to my left. The sea is marvellous and awe-inspiring, with its various moods. Bird life is rich around the estuary. For the first time in my life, I've identified stone chats and rock pipits."

Another book I started reading on this holiday was Thomas Hardy's The Return of the Native. Hardy became one of my very favourite authors. His realistic and, to some extent, pessimistic attitude had some effect on me.

Despite the great pleasures of the holiday, I must have had too much time to think, for my mind was, at times, plagued by conflict. It is incredible that, just on the very point of ending my ministry and beginning another, the thoughts racking my mind were such as they were.

Diary Entry: 25th July

"As I sat, alternately looking through the window and reading Jeanne Franciose's… Prayer and Hope, I thought how incredible Christian belief is. Sometimes the doubt or the question should I say, comes with such force, it knocks the ground from under my feet. Am I on the edge of another serious doubting period? I've felt it coming on for a week or two now—love I am convinced of."

Diary Entry: 27th July

"Sometimes, doubt fills my mind. I even question whether there is a God. I'm afraid of devoting my life to a myth. How do I cope? How should I cope?"

Diary Entry: 31st July

"Paul's love poem was a great comfort this morning. I do still believe in love, even though every other Christian doctrine may be thrown into the melting pot. This week, the thought has again arisen. "How can we be sure of all that Christianity teaches? To read Paul's 'our knowledge and prophecy are partial—we see through a glass darkly.' 'Faith, hope, love abide but the greatest of these is love' 'love never ends,' is a great encouragement.

I can hold onto love, and even if faith burns low, one can still abound in love, the greatest virtue."

Diary Entry: 4th August

"Oh, my conflicting emotions. One minute I may have the highest spiritual aspirations, then the next be full of extremely earthly thoughts. Likewise, I oscillate between faith and dedication to Christ and almost total atheism. I appear to be the most insecure person. In writing that sentence, have I hit on something significant? Insecurity! But is it the other way round? Does my uncertainty and questioning bring with it, the insecurity?"

The time for leaving Wheatley Park was drawing close. One thing that gave me a lot of pleasure was listening to 'Your Hundred Best Tunes' on the radio, most Sunday nights. Classical music was becoming one of my passions tho' I could very rarely attend a live concert.

Diary Entry: Sunday 13th October

"Here I am, for the very last time, listening to 'Your Hundred Best Tunes' in the lounge of 2a Monmouth Road. One of my happiest memories will be of hours spent here on many a Sunday evening."

On this very day, I had taken services at the Methodist church I attended as a boy and a teenager.

Diary Entry:

"Well, today has been one of the happiest of my life. I took the Men's Weekend Service at Hasland Methodist Church. How delightful it was to meet many old friends. Clive and Janice were there with their three children. Miss Pickard, who taught me in the top class of junior school, was present at both services. My singing teacher was there. Others present were Pam Burton, her parents and family. Brenda Key, Mr Lee, the Bembridges of Meakin Street, Mr and Mrs Ellis, and quite a lot of other folk I knew.

Mr and Mrs Slatcher gave me lunch. They were extremely kind.

My theme for the day was Luke 4.18. I applied it as an evangelistic appeal in the morning and as a challenge to the church in the evening.

What a lovely way to spend my last day up here. Tomorrow, I'm off to Oxford."

There is a mention of Grandma Knowles (grandad had died). It is worth quoting as it shows how much grandma thought of me and our family.

Diary Entry:

"We all went to Grandma Knowles for tea. She gave us a slap-up-do. Grandma also gave us £50.00, plus some curtains, a washing basket, pillow slips, duster, cushions, a large tin trunk and a towel. She also gave the children money, crisps and cake. Over the years, I have been so well treated by grandma and grandad.

… I hope she keeps well enough for me to have her in Chesham for a holiday."

Chapter Seven
A WORLD OF UNREALITY OXFORD – MICHAELMAS TERM 1974 ROOM V5 REGENT'S PARK COLLEGE

Before going to Regent's Park, a tutor there had asked me to study Paul Tillich. Cedric Weaver, a 'liberal' clergyman in the next Parish, lent me the first volume of Tillich's theology. (Tillich was a very radical thinker, but I thought it may do me good to read him.) On the evening of leaving Doncaster, my own volumes arrived—just in time! One reason I'd chosen Regent's Park for my term sabbatical was that I wanted to be challenged. In the event, when I arrived there, the 'liberal' tutor had retired and been replaced by an evangelical! What an irony!

Oxford seemed such an unreal world. One could easily get lost in it and evade coming face to face with what was happening elsewhere. Yet, especially at first, it was very enjoyable, and of course, stimulating. It was like nothing I'd ever experienced. Medieval buildings, beautiful grounds, students wearing gowns and, more often than not, riding bicycles. In the college, strange, traditional customs were practiced, such as saying grace in Latin before dinner! Being in such an environment really did seem something of a dream-like existence, with little connection with life outside the university.

What did appeal to me was the opportunity to study in such a place; the services at two Anglican churches also proved very inspiring to me.

John M Hayes

Diary Entry: 15th October

"In consultation with Principal Barrie White, I set off this morning to hear Professor Macquarrie. Oh, it was superb material. I'm going to enjoy these lectures."

These lectures were held in Christ Church where the lecture rooms' walls were covered by famous professors' portraits from past ages. It proved a conducive atmosphere for serious study.

As for the church services:

Diary Entry: 20th October

"What a wonderful Sunday morning! I went, first of all, to the 10.15 a.m. service at St Mary's University Church. H.A. Williams was the preacher (a contributor to 'Soundings'). The service consisted of two hymns, prayers and the sermon. I made notes of the preacher's excellent material."

This last comment shows how far I was moving on in my theological thinking. Some years prior to this, when the radical essays 'Soundings' was published, like my colleagues at Spurgeon's, H.A. Williams would have been regarded as a thinker who undermined 'true Christianity.'

My diary entry continues with another indication of my changing, ecumenical and less fundamentalist position. I decided to attend a 'high Anglican,' which is a Catholic-like service.

Diary Entry: 20th October

"After coffee, I popped around the corner from Regent's to join The Sung Eucharist in Pussey House Chapel.

The service was basically Series II, with minor adaptations. There was a great sense of worship and also community. The preacher was none too good though. I thoroughly appreciated the colour, the vestments, the music, the incense and the candles. It was magnificent.

The Anglicans can certainly teach us a thing or two. It was very noticeable that the congregation participated all the way through."

18:12 p.m.

"The service at New Road Baptist Church tonight was pathetic. Leslie Wenger was the preacher with less than thirty in the congregation... I would like to be used in the training of men for the ministry. This need is so pressing."

(Interestingly, within the year, I was involved through an appointment to the Council of Regent's Park College!)

Halfway through the term, the move to Chesham took place. Margaret and the children would now be in Chesham whilst I completed the sabbatical in Oxford. I did, of course, take a few days off to help with the move.

Diary Entry: 29th October

"My heart is now at 'The Forelands.' We moved into the house yesterday. It seems like a fairy story. Someone said that we must have the grandest Manse in existence. I just can't get over it.

The Georgian house is delightful and the garden fantastic (all two and a half acres of it)! Margaret and the boys are enjoying it as much as I am.

However, am I going to be able to settle down to any work again in Regent's?"

The reality was I couldn't. In retrospect, having the break in Chesham was a mistake. Not only did I fail to settle back in Regent's, but I also suffered sleeplessness and depression. The last five weeks there were unconstructive, wasted.

One highlight, however, was taking the morning service at New Road Baptist Church on Remembrance Sunday. For years, I had never felt comfortable with Remembrance Sunday, but, whilst in Doncaster, I came up with a very good appropriate sermon, which transformed my approach to it. Barrie White, the principal, had given my name to the church—bless him!

Diary Entry: October

"I'm receiving VIP treatment from Barrie White."

My diary entry contains reference to an encounter that, in view of my conflicting feelings and beliefs, is significant.

Diary Entry: 30th October

"This evening, I invited two freshers for a drink in my room. I enjoyed the conversation which developed. Paul, a minister's son from Margate, opened up to us. Recently, he had been through a period of confusion, doubt and questioning. Fortunately, during the Summer, he had begun to find his feet. During the period of 'wandering,' he was driven more and more into his shell. In the church he said, "I felt like an outsider." For him, and for us all, I suppose his experience of doubt was a very lonely affair. He couldn't talk to his father.

We agreed that it is difficult to be a father and a minister to one's own son."

The reference to loneliness is hugely significant. My own conflicts, doubt and failures meant that, for the years in the ministry, I felt, for so much of the time, desperately lonely. Belief is inherently such a personal thing.

Diary Entry: 6th November

"At formal dinner, I sat next to Dr Payne, the General Secretary of the Baptist Union. The subject of healing arose. Both Dr Payne and Barrie White appeared to be quite interested in the subject. Dr Payne spoke of his two heart attacks and the emotional pressures that he believed had contributed to his collapse. I do like it when people share personal experiences. That is real fellowship."

Once or twice, Barrie White had conversations with me about a healing ministry in the church. In my reading of Tillich, I came across insights on a healing ministry.

In November, a bombshell hit us.

Diary Entry: 7th November

"It appears that Margaret is pregnant. Whilst neither of us regret the situation, it does seem a pity that the event has come just now. Margaret

was so happy in the house. She was looking forward to entering fully into things here and, especially, making our home a centre of happiness and blessing. Now, she's feeling sick all day! I am only sorry that just when Margaret seemed to be on her feet and so happy, that the pregnancy occurred. I'm sure that we will enjoy having another baby around the house. Personally, I shall be able to cope much better than I did with any of our present three."

My diary, at this time, illustrates how the world of nature provided increasing delight. Escaping into the natural world brought some calm to my troubled soul.

I was in the study in the Manse.

Diary Entry: 9th November

"Sitting here, overlooking the garden is a delightful experience. The grounds outside are like paradise to me. Already this morning, I've seen wrens, bluetits, a robin and a pied wagtail around the mulberry bush. I wonder what Margaret's father will say when he sees this place."

Another indication of my seeking perpetual recognition and respect.

Diary Entry: 12th November

"We had a beautiful afternoon here in Oxford, and the sun drew me outside for a while. The riverbank is peaceful—hardly a human being around. Bird life is prolific. To my great delight, I was able to observe, for several minutes, a kingfisher. Four times I watched him dive into the water for fish. It is the first time I've identified a kingfisher, although I may have caught a glimpse of one in Sandall Beat Wood in Doncaster, where I often walked."

In view of its importance to me, I should have mentioned Sandall Beat Wood when relating life in Doncaster. The nature reserve was a huge wetland area, adjoining the racecourse, to which I frequently resorted. The place was teeming with birds. Hundreds of, mainly, small trees provided interest too. (I have, all my life, had a respect for and love of trees.)

Beside Tillich, other books were studied on my sabbatical. My tutor recommended a classic R. Niebuhr's The Nature and Destiny of Man. Another book which was easily devoured was John Taylor's The Go-Between God. This book had a profound influence on sermons at Trinity.

There were certainly benefits from being at Regent's and moments of fulfilment and pleasure. The only pity is that I stupidly wasted so much of it!

Diary Entry: 25th November

"The Oxford experience is turning out to be a personal disaster. The loneliness... the shadow side is still there... The trouble is I don't know what to do. God help me! Above all, enable me to protect my sweetheart and to cherish her indeed."

During the time in Oxford, I addressed Graham Dow's group on healing. Graham was chaplain of a university college whom I'd met through the VMTC. The morning after this meeting, James, one of the group members, called to ask if some help could be given to his wife. We arranged a prayer counselling appointment for 17th December in the Forelands.

Diary Entry:

"Margaret and I will work together on this assignment."

And so, I left the unreal, surreal world of Oxford, for the life in the town of Chesham in Buckinghamshire.

Chapter Eight
A DISASTROUS MARRIAGE TRINITY BAPTIST CHURCH, CHESHAM

A disastrous marriage. No, not the personal one, but the one between minister and church. After the very first evening service, I told Margaret that I'd made a mistake. The church and me were a poor match. The congregation, especially the evening one, was a marked contrast to Doncaster; it was small 'dead' and old. Whatever was to be done?

Diary Entry: December 1974

"Oh! What a come down. The service tonight was heavy. I very much missed Wheatley Park. Of course, I knew it would be difficult coming here after Wheatley Park, but I didn't expect that to hit me on my first weekend!"

In the morning, the church had been full, admittedly, with scores of children, as well as adults, but the evening congregation was too much of a contrast for me—almost a physical as well as a psychological shock. It was in stark contrast to the previous day's Induction service. A coach of people came down from Doncaster.

Diary Entry: 15th December

"Margaret and I were showered with gifts, kisses and hugs by our visitors. Oh, what a lovely relationship exists between us. Love was poured upon us." "I feel humble but glad to be here."

The contrast between the Doncaster congregation and the one in Chesham could not have been more stark!

One comfort though was my lovely home.

Diary Entry: 21st December

"The drawing room is simply delightful. Since dinner, we've been listening to the radio. At the moment, Richard Baker is presenting, 'These You Have Loved.'

The children and I enjoyed chopping logs for the fire earlier today and Margaret engaged them in collecting greenery for Christmas decorations. Margaret had already made a marvellous holly wreath for the front door of the house."

This was a lovely happy time for the family.

Diary Entry: Christmas Day 1974

"The children have played happily with their presents. Roger had a comedian set. Just the thing for him! I've noticed lately he does join in adult conversations, and his contributions so often are of a humorous nature."

Despite Roger's dyslexia, which had a major detrimental impact on him, in adult life, we've always found it easy to hold serious, intelligent conversations with him. As a child also, he was so easy, loveable—and still is now, at the time of my writing, in his fifties.

Another interest that provided relief from pressures was the garden.

Diary Entry: Christmas Day

"Yesterday, the children all helped in the garden for a couple of hours… The garden must have been all but totally neglected, but I'm determined to renew it!"

And renew it I did, much to the appreciation of the church members! Because we'd lost Margaret's income from teaching, it was thought that our car might have to go. The church, however, felt it was necessary for me to have a car, and they undertook to more or less pay for its running, much to our relief.

A QUEST FOR MEANING: A Memoir from Pit to Pulpit; from Business to Philanthropy

Life in the church became increasingly stressful, although there was another side to it. Throughout the first four years, before we had to leave The Forelands, the wonderful garden provided pleasure, comfort and inspiration, especially to me, but also to the whole family. Numerous references in my diary, provide evidence of this; I'll quote just a few from the early days.

Diary Entry: 31st January 1975

"The garden is going to be demanding. I enjoyed a couple of hours clearing out the rubbish... The pink blossom on the tree beside the mulberry looks very pretty this morning. Hundreds more snowdrops are coming out all over the garden."

In truth, most of these were in the huge orchard of apple trees, which was eventually sold off to a housebuilder to enable the church to afford to retain The Forelands.

Diary Entry: 1st February

"On the first day of February, the sun is pouring upon the garden. Snowdrops are out in abundance and daffodils are in bud. We've noticed blue tits going into the nesting box. It looks likely that we shall have some young tits born in there this year."

As for the aforementioned bird box, this had been a gift from Eddy Watts, a devoted member of Wheatley Park. He knew that I loved watching birds, and he actually made the box himself.

It was something that, for a while, brought our family together—working in the garden.

Diary Entry: 8th February

"The boys spent the afternoon in the garden with me."

In a 'thank you' letter to our friends at Wheatley Park, I mentioned the garden. *"In the garden, we have one hundred trees and probably the same number of shrubs. It has been grossly neglected, but we are battling on to* recover it. Someone has volunteered to regularly help with the grounds, for which we're truly grateful."

Another reference to the boys in the garden just illustrates what a draw the garden had become to us.

Diary Entry: 23rd April

"Yesterday, we spent some hours outside. Prematurely, we enjoyed some Summer. Margaret enjoyed sunbathing. The trees look beautiful. Andrew and Roger have been a great help in the garden. They are keeping the lawn in good shape so that I am free to do other jobs."

Diary Entry: 26th April

"Tonight, we laid out the lawn for croquette, for the first time. Oh, we did feel posh! We all enjoyed playing. Andrew borrowed a book on the game from the library, so he told us all what to do. He really is marvellous at finding out things."

Speaking of Andrew, I began calling him 'Mr Fix It!' We always felt that he would have made a very competent engineer—how sad, things turned out so differently! Surprisingly, this diary entry, which praises Andrew, went on to be quite derogatory of Roger.

"Roger, on the other hand, reacted like an infant at times, especially when he was losing the game. This week, he had apparently planned to play truant from school, but Rachel told us, so he was foiled in the attempt. Margaret thinks the teacher is working the class hard and he may be reacting to this."

How ironic these comments are! Subsequently, it was Andrew, sadly, who not only played truant but also adamantly refused to go to school. As for Roger, he generally was so well-behaved, I had completely forgotten any of the negative actions noted in my diary!

Besides the garden, the Chilterns' countryside was very beautiful. I soon discovered local paths, and later more lovely parts of the area, like Wendover Woods. As was the case in Doncaster, I was able to enjoy some wonderful walking on my days off. Sadly, I usually walked alone!

A QUEST FOR MEANING: A Memoir from Pit to Pulpit; from Business to Philanthropy

Diary Entry: 11th January

"... the countryside is lovely. Spring is in the air. I noticed green tints on the trees. It was almost like the scene on our painting 'March Sun.'"

This painting by David Shepard, which was bought on our week's holiday in Hastings in 1967, was so evocative of the English countryside. Many a day, I took pleasure in looking at it, and I was sorry to leave it with Margaret, when we parted in 1992.

The Forelands garden was a paradise for birds.

Diary Entry: 12th May

"We've just discovered that a pair of tits are making use of our nesting box."

Diary Entry: 14th May

"The garden is a bird sanctuary. Regularly, we see great, blue and coal tits; green, bull and gold finches; linnets; song and mistle thrushes; and the tree creeper."

Only much later in life, living in the 'Old Rectory' in Brampton with its one-acre garden, have I observed anything as comparable.

Diary Entry: 19th June

"We now have spotted flycatchers nesting in the beams of the Scouts paper storage shed. They are delightful to watch."

I also mention in this diary entry that there was another pair of birds nesting in the garden, but although we thought they were garden warblers, we couldn't be certain.

In these early months, several family members visited. Keith and Joyce, Margaret's sister and her brother-in-law, were probably the first. Margaret's parents visited. Mr Staton was so eager to see the garden, and he didn't waste any time before setting to work in it. Over the short time we were there, he gave advice, especially on what vegetables to grow. Once, he startled me by giving a compliment about my gardening; my, what an accolade by such a gardening afficionado!

My mother and Tom also stayed with us (Tom was the man mother married a year after our dad died.). Mother once brought Grandma Knowles, which I was so pleased about. She loved the house.

Diary Entry: 25th January
"Margaret has come in wearing the maternity dress we bought in Watford on Thursday. She looks very nice."

Perhaps, it was just as well, we were all finding living in The Forelands so pleasurable and that I could find so much joy in nature. It was very much a solace for me because life in the church was, from the start, very stressful. As I've written, my appointment to minister was a 'bad marriage,' which eventually led to divorce. The problem was that my brand of Christianity was not shared by many, perhaps by most of the membership. As a priority, I made a decision to visit every member in their home, within a few days of the Induction. On the membership roll, there were two hundred and forty names. When this was examined, the Deacons removed sixty, bringing the number down to one hundred and eighty! In itself, this revealed that the church leaders had not taken membership of the church seriously, and even after I'd met the residue, it became obvious some of the names left on the roll should probably have been removed. In a letter, everyone on the list was notified that they would soon get a pastoral visit. In fact, during an eight-week period, one hundred and sixty of the one hundred and eighty members were visited—a staggering achievement, considering all other duties that needed to be carried out. In a letter sent out to our 'interested friends' on 11th February, mention was made of these visits. Reference was also made of my shock and disappointment. "The church has not received an evangelical teaching ministry within living memory (with the possible exception of one ministry). Members have been depressed and discouraged of late. Many seem to lack an understanding of even the basics. Some appear to be purely nominal in their Christianity."

There were some, however, who exhibited a spiritual hunger— these lapped up my preaching. The Sunday sermons were my priority.

(Since 1967, that had been the case, and this saw me spending about eight hours in preparation of each of Sunday's two sermons.) Partly because of what was being uncovered by the doctrinal confusion and ignorance of the congregation, I decided to preach on the 'Apostle's Creed' on Sunday mornings, dealing with the basics as it were.

Diary references at this time reveal my shock and dismay.

Diary Entry: 13th January
"I've spent a lot of time visiting today. A bit depressing, it's been!"

Diary Entry: 14th January
"Visitation has again been a sad experience. There are so many old folk, but far more distressing is, so many who don't have much of a clue about Christian faith and life."

Diary Entry: 20th January
"A few people have spoken freely of their spiritual need. One said that she had been 'desperate' and others that they were low, spiritually. Quite a large proportion of folk seem to have a very inadequate grasp of the faith and a limited experience of Christianity... The only consolation for me is that the 'desperate' ones, who deeply feel their weakness, are open to what the Lord may give them through me... It is clear that these are the folk who I must give special attention to... through this group of people, the renewal of the church will come."

On looking now at these comments, it is so clear that though I made them with the best of intentions, I was encouraging the view that only some people in the congregation mattered. In my mind, the seeds were planted that brought about the split, which came about four years later. So, whilst a significant group of folk became what could be called my disciples, a very large section of people were, inadvertently, alienated.

There was certainly a significant number of people who did encourage me though.

Diary Entry: 26th January

John M Hayes

"Five folk expressed interest in joining my 'Basic Christianity' class. Linda West said she wanted baptism. So, after six weeks, we have been given encouragement."

In the end, at least twenty-five people attended, and a number of them were not among those I'd expected. Why didn't I patiently support these folk, who knows what the outcome might have been?

And so, as one large group responded to the preaching, and it should be said a slightly different form of service to that they had become accustomed to, many others were upset, and some began to leave. Quite early on, I introduced 'the giving of the peace,' an ancient church practice that had recently been revived, especially in Anglican and Roman Catholic churches. It was no more than people, prior to taking communion, being invited to greet the person or people beside them with the words 'peace be with you.' As one can imagine, this was just too much for an introverted person! One such, a spinster called Lucy, never returned to a service after the introduction of 'the peace.' My subsequent visit didn't go well; she forcibly threw me out of the house!

Eventually, others drifted away. Quite late on, I was upset when Dr Raymond Holmes and his wife left. (They were the couple who had provided hospitality to Margaret and me, when I'd 'preached' with a view to the Pastorate.) Dr Holmes was not of my theological persuasion, but he was a good man and a doctor who with his wife had been missionaries in Africa. (His father had been a missionary too and had laboured for several years before seeing his first convert. Raymond had been deprived, during his student years. Like some others at lunchtime, he walked outside smoking cheap cigarettes to quell his hunger, because he couldn't afford to eat!) I was pleased when, a few years later, there was a sort of reconciliation, with an exchange of letters.

It wasn't long before my ministry attracted people who were much more sympathetic to my approach, including Margaret Crutchley— the woman I've been married to since 1999 but in love with since

1980! The complexion, especially of the evening congregation, began to resemble more of that in Doncaster.

Very sadly, there continued to be an undercurrent of opposition. A Mrs Pocock ran the Sunday morning Bible class. She and her husband were not deeply involved in the church, except that Mrs Pocock ran a very successful Girls Brigade, as well as the Bible class. It was significant that the young people as they reached a more mature age were not encouraged to graduate by staying in church for the whole service rather than walking out, a little way through, to attend Mrs Pocock's class. At the same time, I couldn't be bothered to take an interest in the Girls Brigade. (Of course, I should have, at least, called in some evenings just to show a little interest. But this didn't happen, and unsurprisingly increased Mrs P's antagonism. She was eventually found out to be criticising me to her tribe, which led to the disastrous split in the church.) In the meantime, living with this caused me a great deal of grief and undermined whatever joy I could have experienced from all the positives.

Diary Entry: 7th July

"I was a bit deflated to see a large crowd of youngsters outside church on Sunday evening. They were going to the Pocock's. It is obvious that many of the girls will not turn up for the regular youth meetings. This nettle will have to be grasped soon or there's going to be trouble."

Unfortunately, 'this nettle' was not grasped soon, and I lived with a very painful situation for more than another three years!

Turning to more pleasant memories, one of the joys was renewing visits with Peter Edwards and Boyd Williams and, of course, their wives: Shelagh and Patricia. Boyd and Trisha had returned from Brazil (where he, a former Conservative, had now become more sympathetic to socialism!) and taken a church in Southall. Peter was in West Wickham. Our former quarterly meetings were resumed to everyone's delight. We certainly encouraged one another.

A number of opportunities to serve outside Trinity arose. My involvement with prayer counselling schools continued.

Very generously and enthusiastically, the Deacons supported my involvement, even though it meant several weeks a year being away from Chesham. In time, several of our lay leaders attended, and the counselling for people like Barbara Eyres and David Dwight was life-transforming. Throughout this time, however, I became increasingly unhappy about the aspect of 'casting out demons' because I didn't really believe in it! I also felt uncomfortable as some of the positive effects of my original counselling session had worn off; some old problems had returned, including a less happy relationship with Margaret. (This was mainly due to my selfishness, which I realised, but that didn't help, it simply made me feel more disappointed and depressed.)

Another outside engagement was being appointed a trustee of a Baptist Minister's Charity Fund. As a result of this appointment, I was elected to the Council of Regent's Park College, Oxford, to represent the fund. Barrie White, the Principal, expressed delight at the appointment; he wanted to see more 'evangelical types' on the council. The position was certainly not onerous, but several visits were made over time, which especially involved helping with the interviewing of potential students.

The important family event in July was the birth of Helen Rebecca. Her arrival brought out some of the best in people and, for a while, seemed to dampen down the undercurrent of dissatisfaction in a significant portion of the church members.

Diary Entry: 17 July

"Helen Rebecca was born at 4.12 p.m. Margaret was taken into the maternity unit for an induced labour. The room was extremely hot, and this caused some distress to Margaret, but the labour was over within two and a half hours. Three nurses were around at the crucial time. The birth wasn't half as messy as I had imagined it would be. It was fascinating to see the baby's head coming down the birth canal, protruding partly, and finally coming out into the world."

Rebecca's was the first birth I'd ever seen; for the births of the other three, I was still lacking in confidence! Continuing with the diary entry:

"The pupil midwife cut the cord, which was wound around the neck, then the baby gave a cry. The whole baby was exposed quickly—it was a girl! We were so pleased because secretly Margaret and I both hoped for a girl.

Winn Howe, a former teacher and member of our church, kindly stood by for the last week or so and today she met the children from school."

Margaret was kept in the hospital for a few days. In the meantime, I was spoilt. Margaret's parents came to collect Rachel for a holiday with them; the boys went off to scout's camp. As for me, several folk provided me with sustenance. The church had made arrangements for Sunday services so that I could provide support for Margaret. My comments on Rachel, at this time, are pertinent.

Diary Entry: 19th July

"Rachel has gone off happily to Chesterfield. What a self-contained (this should have read "a self-assured") person she is. She will bring great pride and joy to us, I'm sure."

My diary contains quite a lot about our cupboards being bare but people being hospitable to me.

Diary Entry: 19th July

"I've made out a menu for myself for tomorrow. All our money is gone so I must make do with what's in the pantry until Tuesday. I'm fed up with the financial situation. Prices have increased 26% since this time last year… David Dwight, bless him, is working behind the scenes to obtain a 15% rise for me, before 1st August.

I must say, people are being most generous and kind to us. I've had lots of invitations for meals, some of which have had to be refused; other folk have done washing and cleaning. People are really marvellous."

Diary Entry: 20th July

"*The Dwights graciously entertained me over lunch, and four hours afterwards, I still feel full!*"

Diary Entry: 21st July

"*Margaret went for her operation today. She felt sore afterwards, but she looked well. Helen Rebecca is a beautiful girl. She is another windy baby.*

Ray and Barbara gave me dinner this evening. They are both coming down tomorrow to give me a hand. Barbara will type or do household chores, while Ray and I trim the Virginia creeper and clean the bedroom windows."

Diary Entry: 25th July

"*Janet Providence invited me to dinner this evening, and I've only just returned after spending a pleasant four hours there. Paul Providence has made his decision to follow Christ.*" (Paul was Janet's teenage son.)

Margaret and Rebecca were kept in hospital for different reasons.

Diary Entry: 25th July

"*Margaret may not be home before Sunday. After the 'op,' she felt rather sore. Rebecca is being looked after by the nurses.*"

One day Margaret's sister, Joyce, put Rachel on the phone from her home in Chesterfield.

Diary Entry: 23rd July

"*Joyce rang up this evening and put Rachel on the phone. Phew! Rachel's powerful personality came over on the telephone. She was obviously thoroughly enjoying herself. I was impressed by the way she expressed herself. Even humour came over clearly.*"

"*Dr Hodge provided me with a fabulous lunch today. Folk are being so good.*" (Dr Hodge was another minister in the town.)

Especially with another mouth to feed, and Margaret, of course, not being able to earn anything from teaching, the financial position was quite difficult. We were, however, given an estate car by Ray Eyres, and we were informed another £3.00 per week was in the pipeline. Then, family allowance would help us.

When Margaret came home, she was pleased with the state of the house and the garden. Once again, she said, "It's like being on holiday living here."

Andrew and Roger returned from the extensive time in camp— Roger with a hedgehog made out of driftwood and Andrew with a pile of rocks and fossils.

Diary Entry: 3rd August

"It's good to be together as a family again; we missed the children when they were away." But there was a drawback.

Diary Entry: 4th August

"The baby is taking up all of Margaret's time."

The baby was having a significant impact on all the family.

Diary Entry: 6th August

"Rebecca gave me some lovely smiles as I held her for a few moments."

Unlike with Andrew, particularly, my confidence had grown, and I very much enjoyed holding the baby. No doubt that's one reason she grew into a very settled child and adult.

Diary Entry:

"The children are all taking a great interest in her. Even, Andrew fed her once. She is certainly surrounded by love."

During these weeks, there were many satisfying family times, and I must have felt more hopeful about marriage and my ability as a father.

Christine Garratt, the youngest daughter of one of our Doncaster friends, came to stay with us for a while. (Andrew was 'sweet on her,' and that the friendship didn't develop and continue, could well have been one of the things that triggered an awful depression in him.)

Diary Entry: 21st August

"Christine has now been with us for a week. She gets on so well with Andrew… We took her to Coombe Hill after lunch. Roger enjoyed flying a paper plane he had made; Rachel walked to the bottom of the hill and up again by herself. Rebecca was mesmerised by the trees."

After feeling that I was a rather neglectful and inadequate father for so many years, my spirits have been lifted by forgotten extracts in my diary, which have jolted my memory.

Diary Entry: 26th August

"All of us, except Margaret, went blackberry picking. We walked up into the fields above our house, then through the farm and down to the bottom of the lane, then up through another farm which brought us out into Trapps Lane. Between us, we gathered over four pounds of blackberries. They have made lovely jam… Altogether, our saving was £2.00."

My mother and Tom were staying with us at this time. Tom, who had never been married before, loved having a relationship with mother's grandchildren.

Diary Entry: 26th August

"Tom has played a lot with the children. At this moment, he is playing a game with them on the grass, outside the study."

Still with the family, it was extremely encouraging that, maybe for the first time in his life, Roger was receiving help at school. He had struggled, and this was at the bottom of what was, from time to time, his naughtiness.

Diary Entry: 3rd September

"Roger is again in Mr Tuffin's class. This is marvellous news for him. He has asked for extra work over the weekends. The confidence barrier while not having been overcome is at least being addressed. Roger's reading has improved tremendously. Ray Eyres says his written work should show improvement by Christmas. How relieved we are that Roger has another year in the middle school; this will give him a good chance to catch up."

Diary Entry 18th September

"*Roger appears to be happy at school. The trouble is he is adept at concealing his feelings.*"

Before rereading the diaries, after many years, I had forgotten how Roger's humour came out as a child.

Diary Entry: 27th September

"*Before turning on the radio, I read Chapter 6 of 'The Hobbit' to Roger and Rachel. In particular, it was Roger who appreciated the humour.*"

Towards the end of the year, the family relationships were still good in contrast to what was happening in church.

Diary Entry: 17th November

"*All the family are becoming avid readers. Roger is ploughing through 'Voyage to Venus' by C S Lewis. His reading progress over the last twelve months has been fantastic. Rachel is reading 'Through the Looking Glass,' and Andrew is discussing with Margaret a birthday present book 'Rocks and Minerals.' It was his birthday yesterday (fourteen), and he received presents, besides a substantial amount of money. We had a good day together. He brought us some ice cream for tea.*"

Writing about these good family times all these decades later has given me some comfort. I've always felt that I neglected the family. That I was too self-absorbed and was a poor husband and father. It must be good that the family have some better memories of me.

Sadly, this happiness with the family in those days stood, at the time, in stark contrast to what was taking place between myself and some element of the congregation, and to this, I must give extensive coverage.

As mentioned earlier, my ministry, almost from the beginning, evoked two opposite responses or reactions. Through the year, giving almost my exclusive attention to preaching/teaching and a narrow form of pastoral care drew out negative feelings in a significant number of people. I did very little social visiting of the old ladies (There were no old men.). My lack of interest in the large Girls Brigade group and the scouts was obvious—I didn't even call in to see what they were doing. A few protested that I didn't give a good 'children's address' at Sunday morning services.

There was simmering resentment that I was flagrantly ignoring traditions and determinedly stamping my style of doing things on the church members. They were right. A more mature, sensible and more assured person would have moved more gently, more patiently. But I couldn't wait! I didn't trust in God; to my mind, it all depended on me! Yes, my ego got in the way. And what havoc was caused! Having since been in business, I can better understand how my stance can be so demoralising, so unnecessarily destructive. But the trouble is, in the Baptist Ministry, ministers are isolated—there is no one to guide or correct, or in any way provide support. It must be recorded, however, that the area superintendent was a decent man and, more than once, showed deep interest.

Diary Entry: 18th October

"The 'Super' called at 8.45 p.m. and he has only just gone. He called to pass on a comment he had heard in Bristol. Someone had said that I was giving the impression that Trinity was hopeless before I came and that this reflected badly on my predecessor. Also, some of our older members, it was reported, were finding my ministry a bit hard to swallow."

I recorded my appreciation of the time he was prepared to give, but nothing, unfortunately, could stop me in my chosen course. Sad to say, one almost relished the conflict; I was going to clear out the 'dead wood' and replace it with something resplendent!

Word was spreading in the town, as it does in the sort of close-knit community like Chesham. At one of our morning town minister's prayer sessions, the Methodist Minister approached the subject of the rumours circulating about Trinity, relating to my ministry.

Diary Entry: 4th November

"At prayers, this morning, we read the words about new wine in old wineskins. Tony Bullock indicated that he had heard something about my

troubles at Trinity..." "We seem to be losing support from a number of members."

Sadly, on looking back, I didn't seem to be very bothered about them, so they were 'dead wood.' Another approach, one that showed a caring about them, may well have brought about a better relationship. Admittedly, it may not have done, and in any case, it would have demanded a display of huge patience; also the expenditure of so much time, which considering all the other demands on me, could not be justified. But, at least, a little more humility and caring on my part may well have achieved something!

A part of my problem was my temper. Even Barbara Eyres gently rebuked me for this.

Diary Entry: 13th November

"Barbara asked me next morning why I react to criticism so irrationally. Peggy Woodly also mentioned it. She said that we all have failings, and the essential thing is to learn the practice of forgiveness."

Of course, the answer to Barbara's question is that despite having great confidence in certain aspects of my work, for example, preaching and counselling, I was all at sea in general pastoral work, like visiting the older members of the congregation and giving talks to children! Instead of speaking openly about these weaknesses to our Deacons, and trying to find a resolution, I hit out because the criticism had struck home and hurt. These flaws in me, which I often asked God to help me overcome without any change occurring, were central in my often questioning whether prayers were even answered or whether there was even a God who could answer prayers. The struggle, which was constant and extremely painful, to become a more mature person often left me in despair and certainly tried my faith to the limit. I was well aware that the troubles in the church could have been avoided, or at least, toned down, if I had gone about things differently. So, the guilt piled up, and the guilt fed depression; the resulting mess adversely affected all relationships, most pertinently with Margaret and the children. I was often angry, critical and snappy. Certainly, nobody could have described me as a 'together person.' Conflict raged inside, almost constantly. In fact, nearly half-way through the following year, another public argument with the Pocock's, revealed my continuing vulnerability.

Diary Entry: 29th May

"The P's greatly upset me again on Monday night, and I stupidly walked out of the meeting after blowing my top. I cannot see my way out of this intractable problem. It would seem that resources are not available within me to cope with the situation. I am worried about it, but, simply, I must trust the Lord to work a miracle. David Orton and David Dwight have been the most helpful. After the Monday incident, David Orton called and stayed counselling me until midnight. Then, as soon as he heard about the incident, David Dwight came round!"

Changing the subject, there were two episodes totally unrelated to the church, which were very special to me, such as I want to record them here.

Whilst still at Wheatley Park, Margaret's sister, who sometimes stayed with us, one day brought her friend Susan. To my delight, I discovered that Susan was the daughter of my boss at Williamthorpe Colliery, none other than Mr Rimmer, who had pointedly asked me if I thought working at a coal mine was really right for me! Just before my transfer to Chesham, Susan had asked if I would preside at the wedding service in Chesterfield she had planned for the following year. Fortuitously, I was able to book the date, which was a Saturday, and then agree to take the following Sunday services in Barnsley Baptist Church. What a hectic weekend! After the wedding reception, I ran over to Whitwell for my sister's son's birthday. My car was then filled with presents for our new baby. They came from my mother and grandmother, mainly. I then called on Joyce, my sister-in-law in Chesterfield—she had more presents! To top it all, Mr Stanton spent another hour cramming as many plants into whatever space was left in the vehicle.

A QUEST FOR MEANING: A Memoir from Pit to Pulpit; from Business to Philanthropy

My hosts in Barnsley had been warned of the late arrival, and I duly arrived at 9.30 p.m. Goodness me, what energy I expended that day. Fortunately, I slept well and arose refreshed for the two arranged services.

But it was the wedding that was the centre piece of the weekend for me. Here I was taking a wedding service for the daughter of a man I so much liked and respected—the man who, as my boss at the time seventeen years previously, led me away from a career in coal mining to one in the church. How emotional I felt—the day was one of those very, very special days for me.

Diary Entry: 2nd June 1975

"The wedding went well. Mr Rimmer remarked that he had never seen so many happy faces in church before. A number of folk warmly thanked me for the service and the address."

The other special event was, by contrast, a funeral. It seems almost sacrilegious to refer to it as a happy event but it was. Stephen Hall was a member of our Methodist Church in Whitwell. It was Stephen who, indirectly, pushed Margaret and me to marry, when he offered us his house, fully furnished, for twenty-five shillings a week! Over the years, we had kept in touch; in fact shortly before he died, all our family visited him when he was bedridden, in his brother's house. Characteristically, out came presents for everyone! Such a gentle, lovely man, a porter at Boots Chemist, so unassuming, but by his goodness, he left a mark on many people. Well, he died in December 1975, and there was absolutely no chance of our not attending the funeral.

Diary Entry: 4th December

"Yesterday, Stephen Hall was buried in Whitwell Cemetery. Over two hundred people attended the service in Portland Street Chapel. I met old friends, including David and Chris Lee who had come over from Grimsby.

Stephen had arranged the detail of his funeral service. The choir sang 'Homeland,' the congregation sang three great Methodist hymns (M.H.B. 677; 110; 877). A collection was made for the organ fund; no flowers were given apart from those that Stephen himself had ordered and paid for.

Everybody was invited to a lovely tea in the hall, which had also been paid for by Stephen.

What a moving occasion it was and what a tribute to one of the Lord's saints.

I was so grateful to Ray Cluroe for writing to tell me of Stephen's death and so glad to be there for the funeral."

Trinity life continued very much as it had in our first year there. The divisions in the church, if anything, got worse. At the same time, the dedicated core of people grew and thus changed the character of services on Sundays. For example, one event that made an impact was our Renewal weekend. Several couples from Wheatley Park came down, simply to share their Christian experience with the Trinity folk. My intention and hope was that something of the spirit of Wheatley Park would rub off, and it did!

Diary Entry: 24th May 1976

"People are looking towards the weekend now with great anticipation. About seventy have registered, with fifty-five of them participating in the house meetings. Very few of our over seventies members are joining in the weekend."

Diary Entry: 29th May

"The Church Weekend got off to a good start. A house meeting is in progress in the Longroom, and while Margaret participates, I'm, in theory, looking after the children… Andrew has gone to another house meeting."

(It grieves me now to read this extract concerning Andrew. He quite clearly did participate in some church activities before his personal crisis.)

Diary Entry: Bank Holiday Monday 1976

"I still feel in a daze. What happened yesterday was so unexpected. After two excellent services, over seventy people remained for a Fellowship hour, which was led by Michael Dwight. I sat in wonder at what happened. A

church was transformed before our very eyes. People were released to testify, pray, praise, sing and love.

God has done great things.

About thirty-five set off at 9.45 a.m. for a twelve-mile walk. Arnold Baines, who had planned the route, led the party. Over forty others are taking a four-and-a-half-mile route this afternoon. Another dozen or so are looking forward to a short coach tour. All three groups should be at Kimble Free Church for a 4 o'clock tea. The weather is perfect for walking."

Margaret and I began to open our home; now and again, we invited quite a significant number of members to 'Friday at the Forelands.'

Diary Entry: 30th April

"In a few minutes, people will begin to arrive for the third 'Friday at the Forelands.'"

Following the transformational Church Weekend, the next two years contained excitement and sadness in almost equal measure, for the family, the church and for me personally.

As for the family, the arrival of Helen Rebecca changed a great deal. Margaret was unable to engage with the church quite as much as she would have liked, for instance, most Sunday evening services were missed; obviously, it wasn't possible for me to babysit! This, I believe, upset her. She did compensate, to some extent, by opening our home and thus meeting lots of people. I cannot escape the feeling, however, that she may have resented the restrictions imposed on her by a new baby's arrival. As usual, I was insensitive to her needs, and Margaret, being Margaret, kept quiet. Perhaps, this was another example of what Peter Edwards said about her, many years later: "Well, Margaret seemed to live through you John." Inadvertently, this meant there was no real partnership, no talking through a need of hers, and no opportunity to come close together by sharing and caring more. As ever, I felt that it was impossible to really know my wife as she seemed so private, shy and vulnerable to being abused. Throughout this time, I was not unhappy, altogether, but the marriage was nowhere near as strong as either of us would have liked. Eventually, some help was forthcoming when Margaret returned to teaching, but I'll come to that later, as her appointment only came at the very end of this period, coinciding with the traumatic events of the Summer and Autumn of 1978.

Rebecca was a lovely baby who developed quickly. Being an intelligent and confident creature, people responded warmly to her as folk had done with Rachel in Doncaster. All the children enjoyed playing with her, so although her arrival brought with it a huge amount of extra work for Margaret, it also brought a great deal of joy to the family.

Rachel wasn't extremely bright but one remembers her teacher in the junior school saying that she was good at maths. Also, she did pass her eleven plus, as Andrew had done. I've found references in my diary to some of her achievements. One such refers to a practical skill.

Diary Entry: 18th May 1977

"Rachel has come top in a countrywide embroidery competition. We are going to see her work today, which is on display in Aylesbury. Apparently, the Queen saw it yesterday! Over one hundred schools were involved in the competition, so we're really proud of Rachel."

In some respects, Roger, who had suffered quite a few setbacks, also received some encouragement in educational attainment. Before transferring to the secondary school, he took to one of his teachers who had taken an interest in him. At first, he also settled in well at the secondary school.

Diary Entry: 2nd September 1976

"Roger has enjoyed the first two days at his new school. A craft teacher exclaimed 'splendid' when he saw something Roger had modelled in clay. How wonderful it would be if Roger really enjoyed school from now on."

Sadly, this was not to be. Due to his dyslexia, academic work was a struggle. Eventually, however, his artistic ability came to be recognised to such an extent that his arts teacher told me that Roger should be sent to art college on his leaving school.

One thing Roger enjoyed was playing chess, and although I was hopeless at it, the game was something that brought us together. Usually, my opponent won but I did enjoy playing; it was very relaxing, requiring intense concentration thereby diverting one's mind from everything else.

Now, coming to Andrew. For him, this period of time was all downhill! At one time, I used to feel guilty about dragging him down to Chesham halfway through a school term. This must have inevitably upset him. He would also miss the liveliness of a large group of people in Wheatley Park. Just like me, it would have been a huge culture shock, transferring to Trinity. Whatever the cause of his troubles, he certainly experienced difficulties. His conflicts first manifested themselves by refusing to go to school. This resulted in our having meetings with the caring headmaster, who, one morning, came to our house and tried to persuade Andrew to get out of bed! His efforts were abortive—in truth, almost everyone who endeavoured to help Andrew was met with defeat. At the root of the problem was an inability for anyone to even begin to understand the lad. At one point, Andrew did complain of bullying by a teacher but no one imagined that this was the root of Andrew's actions. Our GP, against our wishes, once sent him to a psychiatrist but that drew a blank. Then, the educational psychologist became involved. Sometimes, I accompanied Andrew to her house, walking or partly running there. The sessions drew a complete blank. Once, Bob and Hilary Alexander, a young couple from the church, took Andrew in, and for a while, Andrew cooperated and attended school.

Unfortunately, the trouble led to violence. In the early days, there were times, when trying to persuade him to get out of bed, he turned violent. On one Sunday afternoon, when trying to talk some sense into him, he attacked me. A few hours later, my injuries were visible to the congregation, and there was the perpetrator sitting right in front of me! Another time, as the family was sitting around the dinner table, he threw a tantrum and upset the table, causing the younger children to be afraid. As for school, the head presented an ultimatum, which I recorded.

Diary Entry: 27th January 1977

"The headmaster has presented an ultimatum. By Monday, Andrew has to agree to boarding school, Cestrum or Chesham High, or go to court! I'm afraid he is so stubborn, and we can see him being put into care in the end."

It was after this warning that the Alexanders took him under their care. Andrew only had a year and a half before he could leave school at sixteen, but in the event, he only sporadically attended, and one can say he left school by default. Andrew's difficulties and the frustration of not knowing how to help him did nothing for my confidence. It became yet another source of inner turmoil as I wrestled with guilt, as if I hadn't got enough of that already!

Despite all this turmoil at home, Margaret was happy to keep open house. One day, it was recorded that thirty-five people had spent some time with us; there were people at breakfast, lunch and dinner, besides a group meeting in the evening. I'll quote from a Christmas newsletter sent out in 1976.

Diary Entry:

"The Forelands continues to be the nerve centre of the church. We literally keep open house. Last week must have been a record, between Friday breakfast and Saturday tea, a period of thirty-two hours, we received thirty callers. These were church members who called for pastoral reasons or on business. On the Friday, ten of us sat down for lunch together. Once a month, we keep a special open house from 6 p.m. Some people bring their tea, others arrive later with their children."

On top of all this, many members of our family as well as many friends, especially from Doncaster, came to stay with us. Until I recently consulted my diary, I'd forgotten how frequently we were 'invaded.' My mother and Tom made several visits and twice with Grandmother Knowles. Margaret's parents were often here as were her sister Joyce and husband Keith. John Sanderson, the former church secretary of Wheatley Park, now a minister, stayed with us a few days whilst attending the Baptist Union Assembly in London. Marie

Snook, another Doncaster friend, stayed for a weekend. Others too, including Gordon and Ruth Bennett, Martin and Linda Chadwich. A young minister too, for whom I'd acted as 'Senior Friend', called one day, and so, the list goes on. Those mentioned are only a few of the people who enjoyed our hospitality.

Somehow, in the midst of all this, we still managed to find fulfilment and relaxation in the garden. A new venture was growing things. We already had cooking apples and mulberries, but we moved over to vegetables as well. The time came when half the garden was sold to a developer for a select housing development, that's when we lost all those apple trees! When the builders came in, they were disruptive and sometimes noisy, but, on the whole, failed to disrupt us seriously. Whether it was anything to do with this, I'm not sure but Margaret was often sickly. She rarely seemed to enjoy robust health. My diary is full of references to this. I also frequently contracted a cold. As for Margaret's weakness, this was another issue that prised us apart. Regularly, out of sheer necessity, but also because it gave me so much pleasure, I would take a walk. Margaret's illness and/or caring for the baby ruled out the possibility of her joining me. And so, such a hugely important part of my life couldn't be shared with Margaret, or at least not very often. One diary reference provides a clue to my feelings of frustration.

Diary Entry: 14th April 1977

"Margaret has begun to feel ill, and I don't feel too good either. Oh, what a family!"

Personally, I've never been a good patient, and showing sympathy to others in their suffering isn't exactly my forte. I could show impatience with Margaret when she felt weak. All of us, however, found solace and joy in the garden. We eventually found that what we at first called snakes, more accurately, were actually called 'slow worms.'

Diary Entry: 30th March 1978

"This evening, I watched two slow worms fighting, or were they mating, on the path below the kitchen garden steps. There have been several sightings of slow worms this year."

In the same extract, mention is made of both Margaret and Roger working on the garden. More than two years after our arrival on the scene, the reference indicates how much 'The Forelands' garden continued to command our interest and provide delight.

Another example of this was in April 1976.

Diary Entry: 17th April 1976

"We had tea on the lawn, much to Rebecca's delight, after a hard afternoon's gardening. Roger helped to plant thirty broad bean plants from Chesterfield; the first veg to be planted in our new kitchen garden. Andrew took four loads of topsoil to Norah Sheath and planted flowers in the sunken garden. He also put more weedkiller down on the paths, after tea. I planted a row of forget-me-nots, some of which came from the Sheath's. A beautiful afternoon but we need rain desperately."

One day, meditating on how beneficial it was to have such a garden, I listed some of the benefits felt by myself.

Diary Entry: Bank Holiday Monday 1976 (8.10 p.m.)

"I worked hard in the garden till teatime. It is worth recording the benefits I derive from gardening.

1. Good physical exercise
2. Recreation
3. Good food
4. Some financial benefit
5. A degree of self-sufficiency
6. The joy of creating beauty

A valuable asset. Twelve hours a week is not too much to give for all this benefit."

A diary entry three days later provides a very accurate summary of my emotional connection, both with the garden and with the natural world, generally.

Diary Entry: 1st September 1976
"An exquisitely beautiful morning. Autumn, my favourite season, has arrived. Trees are turning colour; the first leaves have fallen. The watery sun has lost its burning heat and dazzling brightness. Recent rain has refreshed the garden taking away the barren look of the parched lawns."

So many years later, Autumn remains my favourite season: 'season of mists and mellow fruitfulness.'

Roger remembers me walking around the house uttering these words. He has now volunteered to recite Keats poem at my funeral!

In contrast to all this bliss, my state of mind throughout the years continued to be in turmoil. I was ashamed of the perceived and the actual failures. These were undermining married bliss, as well as undermining all the positive things happening in the church. The church leaders made clear their concern. They saw some of the blatant faults and realised that there was something unsettling me. What they couldn't know about was the continuing conflicts I suffered about Christian doctrine, or even sometimes, the serious questioning of even the existence of God. And, neither could they see my materialistic ambitions, of which I was ashamed, as a minister supposedly devoted to God's service and, theoretically, was willing to embrace relative poverty. Guilt, guilt, guilt! The diary references to my chaotic emotional state are so numerous; it is embarrassing. They reveal how self-absorbed I had become. There's little wonder that my family life and my relationship with Margaret were so disappointing. Margaret put up with too much, yet if she had stood up to me, I doubt if it would have made any difference.

The lay leaders of the church were fully aware of some of my flaws; they tried to help.

John M Hayes

Diary Entry: 27th August 1976

"*David and Barbara called on Monday to explain that they had been concerned about the state of my mind since the 'Pocock' affair. The Deacons had been asked to pray for me, and Barbara had consulted Hugh Hutchman.*" (He was one of the Board Members of the VMTC, whom I worked with on the prayer counselling schools.) "*I'm more than grateful for their concern. They said that they had noticed how much more relaxed I appeared since the Fellowship Weekend.*"

They were right; there had been a significant improvement of my mood since then, but it didn't last.

Diary Entry: 27th January 1977

"*Again, I'm down in the dumps. For a whole week, I've let things slip… The mind is obsessed again—doubts abound, depression prevails.*"

There was a profound irony that whilst I professed to be passionately committed to the 'renewal' of the church, in my own mind, grave doubts swam around about even the fundamentals of Christianity, and I personally failed to live up to it. Is there any wonder, life for me was so stressful?

A diary reference illustrates how this state of affairs was so destructive of our marriage, even as early as 1976.

Diary Entry: 1st October 1976

"*Yesterday was dreadful. As the day wore on, I became increasingly depressed and, in the end, blew up with Margaret. It seems to me that I'm under considerable strain, and, perhaps, have come nearer to the breaking point than I'd realised. Margaret comes into it because she has been under pressure too, and although I've tried to support her in practical ways, I feel deprived of the kind of release and support that a woman is supposed to give to her husband.*"

Many years later, on looking back, I could see that although Margaret was a good person who really cared and would do anything she could to please me, she was such a different personality to mine. I sometimes found her boring; she was not often able to express a zest for life, which has always been part of me, and recognised as such by so many friends, even in all but the darkest of days. It does, of course, take two to tango!

Just one more reference, made towards the end of this period of time, very clearly demonstrates how debilitating my emotional state continued to be.

Diary Entry: 24th March 1978

"Only ten pages of diary written in six months. That shows my condition clearly enough. I only carry on here because of the conviction that I must. I'm not at all fit to minister, yet it is better to carry on, though so unworthy, than resign. By God's grace, the people here will grow, in spite of me, if I only carry on. To resign would leave them bereft."

Fortunately, episodes of pleasure and joy appeared from time to time. Meeting up with Peter and Shelagh Edwards and Boyd and Trisha Williams, who settled in Southall on their return from Brazil, was always something to eagerly participate in. Whole days were taken up with coffee, lunch and tea. Eventually, all of us had children, in all nine, so the gatherings were lively. Margaret benefitted from the women's friendship, whilst, for me, it was so encouraging to share with Peter and Boyd what was going on in our churches.

Another thing that sometimes lifted me out of negativity was the connection with Regent's Park College. Sometimes, I was engaged in the interview of an applicant for a place at the college.

Towards the end of 1976, Regent's offered me a student assistant for a year. Myra was the daughter of a popular minister; she was also extremely personable. It was a joy to have her working with me a few hours a week. (Of course, she spent most of her time studying in Oxford.) The Deacons and, in fact, the whole congregation took to her.

Diary Entry: 3rd April 1977

"Myra Findlay took the hospital service this morning and later presided over our morning worship. It helped relieve my load; she is an extremely mature girl—belying her twenty years."

John M Hayes

Diary Entry: 5th April 1977

"Myra led the study this evening, so Margaret was able to attend (thirty-five were present)."

Going over to Oxford was always enjoyable. Apart from anything else, it was a beautiful drive. But Barrie White's welcome of me and encouragement gave me a huge confidence boost.

Diary Entry: 4th February 1978

"Yesterday saw me at Regent's interviewing John Weaver and John Wilson for the Baptist Ministry. Both good material.

On this visit, I was able to meet up with Charles Garrett, a good friend and former member of Wheatley Park, who, as a very mature student, was training at Regent's for the ministry."

"After dinner, Charles took me to his new home. Ruth was her usual delightful self. The three of us chatted enthusiastically for two and a half hours. Charles cycles to college. He looks slimmer and healthier than he used to. Apparently, his studies are going well."

Following on from Myra, Chris, a very different kind of person, was appointed as my temporary assistant. He was a large, solid chap who, like Myra, became very popular with all of us. (One important thing I learned from him—allow the boiling water to settle down before pouring it onto the coffee beans, unlike tea, where one pours on the boiling water!) Chris was with us at the time of the great church crisis, which I shall be coming to soon.

Once again, though, a reference to music ought to be made. The borrowed equipment and few classical records were such a solace. Beethoven's 5th was frequently played and never failed to at least temporarily lift the spirits and help motivate me. But, unfortunately, the simmering troubles in the church came to a head in the Summer of 1978, and nothing was the same thereafter.

At a Deacons meeting, it came to light that Grace Pocock was making critical remarks about me to the young people over whom she had such a hold. Following a discussion, the decision was made to take action—probably to even remove her from leading the Bible class.

Here is a record of it from my diary.

Diary Entry: 6th June 1978

"Last night, the Deacons decided to ask for Grace Pocock's resignation from the Bible class leadership. I immediately felt relief. It was as though a heavy weight had been lifted from my back. I also had the best night's sleep for a long time. Obviously, the Pocock troubles had burdened me even more than I'd realised.

We now feel that a major obstacle to progress in the church has been removed."

Oh, I wish! The matter took a long time to be resolved, and when, in the Autumn, it finally was, it didn't go my way!

In the meantime, a number of things happened to cheer us up.

First of all, in June, I attended a Spurgeon's College annual conference, which one normally did. It was so encouraging to renew contact with quite a number of former students whom I'd been in college with. The preachers were also very much appreciated. One thing I was very serious about, in the Charles Spurgeon tradition, was preaching.

Charles Haddon Spurgeon was, perhaps, the most renowned of Victorian preachers, even Queen Victoria sometimes attended services to hear him. It is unsurprising, therefore, that I believed so strongly in the power of preaching to change lives. It is just a fact that my preaching had achieved such, both in Wheatley Park and in Trinity. It was, sadly, partly this that upset other people so much!

Following what was by now the family tradition, we took a fortnight's holiday in the Isle of Wight. Our location was a large thatched cottage in Steephill Cove. The cove was discovered on our very first holiday there in 1968, but this was the first time we had actually rented the cottage, which was right on the beach. It was to be our last holiday on the island, however.

Whilst away, our student, Christopher, covered for me. "He has a good pulpit ministry," my diary records.

Another little break was spent in Chesterfield, and I don't need my diary to jolt my memory that we took Granma Knowles out to Bakewell for dinner. I can well remember the happy event. On this visit, the diary does remind me, Margaret and I made the decision to consider buying a house in Chesterfield.

It is fascinating that on another visit to Chesterfield I made a note in my diary that…

Diary Entry:
"I would like to live, one day, in either Old Brampton or Walton."

When I reread these words in April 2020, I felt a strange, almost, magical sensation. At this moment, I'm still living in Old Brampton, and have been for twenty-one years, but in a few months, I'll be living in Walton, in a brand-new house! Wow—eerie!

Another very important development that had an immense impact on our family life was Margaret's return to teaching.

Diary Entry: 27th August 1978
"Margaret begins school on the 12th. I'm looking forward to receiving extra money. It appears that she will earn in the region of £3,500 per annum."

Diary Entry: 12th September 1978
"Margaret has begun at Heatherton House."

Diary Entry: 29th September 1978
"Margaret received her first month's pay from Heatherton House—£288.00. Staggering! My basic monthly pay is precisely £100.00 less than this."

Margaret was happy at school, a private one where there was less 'political correctness' and bureaucracy. The significance of the extra money is illustrated by another diary reference.

Diary Entry: 17th October 1978

"We are looking forward to spending extra cash. One half of the extra will be saved mainly through insurance policies. At the moment, we still owe £150.00, and the current account is £30.00 overdrawn. I'm sick and tired of the financial situation and can only hope we never get into such a mess again!"

At last, the Pocock crisis came to a head at a church A.G.M. It was devastating. What none of us in leadership realised was that the Pocock allies had been contacting all the people who had recently left the church but who were still on the membership roll. Their supporters had been galvanised. Many of them hadn't even been to church at all, in my time. Of course, all the disaffected saw the crisis as an opportunity to possibly get rid of me! In opposition to what the majority of the Deacons wanted, a motion was submitted that only the Sunday school superintendent should be able to appoint or dismiss the Bible Class leader. This motion was passed. For me and those who supported me, this was devastating. I was placed in an invidious position. But, in the end, it wasn't left for me to act. Those who supported me decided the solution they preferred was for a split to take place. I was invited to be minister of the breakaway group, which incidentally consisted of most of the very active members. This outcome was certainly not what I'd either expected or sought, but it did seem the only way to save my ministry in Chesham. This group then began to hold Sunday services in a community centre. House meetings were held during the week. Of course, we couldn't indefinitely live in The Forelands, but a £10,000.00 loan from the new church, which was named the St Andrew's Fellowship (because St Andrew's Day fell in the month that we started meeting), enabled us to buy a semi-detached house in a nice area of the town. It was fortuitous that Margaret had started work, and the church provided another pay-rise, so we took a mortgage for £22,000.00 on 64 Berkely Avenue.

At first, although the last thing, I would have wanted was a split church, the St Andrew's group gave me a lot of happiness.

Diary Entry: 24th March

"*St Andrew's is giving us great joy. Congregations, especially on Sunday mornings, are excellent, and a lovely atmosphere prevails in the hall.*"

Very soon, however, I began to feel there was a lack of work and 'the devil finds work for idle hands.' My position at Regent's Park was, naturally, lost, and all contact with the Baptist Ministers in the area and with the Baptist Union was broken. The days often dragged.

Diary Entry: 26th September 1979

"*The other day I told Barbara there was insufficient work for me in St Andrew's.*"

My intention, then, was to seek a part-time job, but when this was mentioned to the Deacons, they were dead against the idea. I often wonder if things, ultimately, would have turned out very differently had they shown more sympathy with the idea. One reason it would have done me good was that it would have kept me out of mischief! As Thomas Carlyle said, "Work is the grand cure for all maladies that afflict the soul of man." (After many years of quoting this aphorism, I read a biography of Carlyle. Thereafter, I refrained from quoting it because, although Carlyle was a worker, he was, in fact, a thoroughly unhappy and unpleasant man!)

My underemployment became almost intolerable; I am not the sort of person who likes to sit around.

Diary Entry: 7th November 1979

"*A very large problem at the moment is underemployment. Some days there is nothing to do. There are now only fifty-seven members of St Andrew's, most of whom are not available during the day. I have taken no funerals or weddings this year. There are no men's clubs or sisterhoods at which I'm expected to speak. Committees have been abandoned— even Deacons and church meetings are held less frequently. I only write quarterly, instead of monthly, for the church magazine. There has to be a way out of this too-easy life. When Rebecca begins to stay at school all day, I shall have to find a job. At the moment, she absorbs a few of my hours each day.*

My intention is to work hard on the house this winter and put the garden straight in the spring and summer, then, hopefully, some employment will be provided. Even if the church trebled in size, it would not greatly alter my position."

All this time on my hands didn't do anything for my emotional life—and naturally, had a very negative effect on our marriage and my faith.

Diary Entry: 13th December 1979

"A deep sadness has filled my heart for months now. I live with Margaret as with a stranger. God seems far away, almost unreal. Is he real? Does God exist? I wonder! It is sad that I am unable to provide the church with the leadership it deserves. A year has passed since our separation from Trinity... thank God the folk do not know their pastor—it would break some of their hearts. It almost breaks mine. There is no way out.

I am so angry—with myself. Most of all about my relationship at home. God, am I angry!"

Walking, especially in the country, continued to provide solace. Three of the four children were also developing well, to my delight. Roger, in some ways, was transformed. In April of this year, he came home from school very pleased with himself; he had won first prize in a book cover design competition. Obviously, his artistic ability is becoming evident to a wider circle. I began to have a deep respect for Roger as my diary attests.

Diary Entry: 23rd October 1979

"Roger is growing into a nice person. Since the summer, he has learned to communicate freely with adults. He has also smartened up and looks a handsome lad. Several people have commented on his progress."

Another confirmation of his progress came when another teacher commended him for his English and actually said that "he has a natural ability with words." I was gobsmacked and felt so proud of the lad!

Just before Christmas, when I was feeling so low again, chatting to Roger was a bright spot, particularly when he referred to Margaret and me as 'his friends.'

Diary Entry: 13th December 1979

"Roger is the bright spot in the family. He is such a lovely chap—full of kindness. He often sits and chats away to us, especially about his schoolwork. The other day, in a roundabout way, he referred to his parents as 'his friends.'"

Rachel also seemed to be thriving at Chesham High, even though, apart from maths, she didn't appear to be academic. She was a popular pupil, perhaps, because she was so friendly, outgoing and sociable. (Certainly, in adult life, these qualities were prominently on display. She lived in Matlock for many years, and whenever I walked with her, through the town, lots of people would greet her, often enthusiastically.) One day, she returned home from Chesham High very excited; she had been appointed house captain. We were delighted, though not entirely surprised, as Rachel had always been such a people person.

As for Margaret, at this time, I just felt a disappointment with her. On holiday, at Lee Abbey, a Christian holiday centre, I wrote some negative comments.

Diary Entry: 12th August 1979

"This is a fabulous place—the setting breathtaking. We are so glad to be here. Margaret is sick. I think that she has been ill on every holiday we've experienced. She was complaining of stomach trouble last week and now she is in trouble again. Since 4 a.m., she has been confined to bed.

I know it says a lot about me, but I do feel angry. Why is Margaret so weak—why is she so often tired—why is it that life is so dull with her?

The marriage is a shambles—we hardly communicate. We are a failure spiritually, finding it almost impossible to praise or pray together. Lord, I so want it to be different!—that's why I'm angry isn't it? —angry because of disappointed hopes, shattered dreams and unfulfilled longings.

A QUEST FOR MEANING: A Memoir from Pit to Pulpit; from Business to Philanthropy

It is almost as if Meg cannot enjoy herself, can't let go. She seems to need to be under control and therefore never lets her hair down.

Oh, if only a new beginning could be made—but Meg doesn't seem to be capable of responding. Is it any wonder that I desire others? I do long for a more mature, lively and interesting woman—can't help it!

For feeling this way, I despise myself."

This passage from the diary is so poignant; it goes to the heart of our personal agony. I feel as I've always felt that I was far too hard on Margaret. Looking back now, after so many years, I think the diary extract reveals that our marriage was nearly over, because we were so different and were unable to share and enjoy the differences; at the same time, we found it so difficult to truly communicate. The marriage was, probably, beyond being salvaged. What happened nine months later demonstrates this at least to me if to no one else.

Only one thing was more sad, or at least as sad, was Andrew's deterioration. Despite people offering a temporary home, which he took up, his anger, depression and seeming hate of me only deepened, leading to several extremely violent exchanges. He left school at sixteen, tried several jobs and found different lodgings but continued to plague us until, after one very dangerous encounter, he ended up in Oxford prison for a few nights. A Mrs Kent shortly gave him refuge, and with her, of course, he was 'as good as gold.' For a while, he lived with a family from another church, but just before the criminal incident, he wheedled his way back and actually slept in the study floor of 64 Berkely Avenue. The last time he did this, he hit Margaret across the face and broke a tooth; she was off school for two days recovering. Rather than relate all the incidents, I'll leave it there.

My depression, unhappiness and stress left me vulnerable to temptation.

Chapter Nine
MY LIFE TURNED UPSIDE DOWN

On 20th May 1980, having arranged to call on Margaret Crutchley, ostensibly to offer pastoral support due to her concern about her husband falling away from the church, I told her that I'd fallen in love with her. These romantic feelings had been aroused after several such 'pastoral' visits. Although Maggie, as I soon chose to call her, was surprised and shocked, within days she had fallen for me. In very different ways, each of our marriages was heading for the rocks; Maggie's husband, Gordon, was threatening to leave her as soon as the three children had finished education!

The encounter, on this day, was to lead to both of our lives being turned upside down. It eventually resulted, for me, in resignation from the church and the adoption of atheism. It also, sometime later, led to my establishing a successful business, which resulted in me becoming very affluent. After a twelve-year lapse, I was reunited with Maggie, and we eventually married. Life turned upside down indeed!

At the time our relationship began, we were both sincere believers, I, of course, was still a minister. Although, because of our traditional Christian views of sex and of marriage, we were restrained in our relationship, despite very strong sexual appeal; in reality, neither of us could think of much else but our romantic entanglement. Throughout the summer, encounters took place frequently, but we still refrained from sexual intercourse. Eventually, I found it impossible to continue with the church responsibilities, especially preaching, without feeling very uncomfortable indeed. Perhaps, I was heading for a nervous breakdown. Something, obviously, had to give.

By October, one or two people, including Margaret, were aware of what was happening. A few of the Deacons came to see me; they were, at face value, non-judgemental but wanted me to take time off to try to sort myself out. Maggie was visited by Barbara Eyres and a young, sensitive Deacon, and thereafter she was terrified about ever meeting me. We agreed not to pursue the relationship, but Maggie wanted to seal our true love by having some time, just for once, to make love. Before her meeting with Barbara and Chris, we arranged for her to come to 64 Berkely Avenue, and we spent some time making love. Then, we parted and assumed that would be the end. In most ways, it was, at least for the next twelve years!

To be honest, Maggie and I had struggled for weeks to control ourselves. It had become obvious to each of us that we couldn't carry on, yet still, we couldn't stay away from each other. Margaret had been aware of what was happening for some time and made a huge effort to help me, and to save our marriage. My diary contains many references to her gallant efforts, and to the fact that, at one level, I too wanted to avoid disaster. Several times, I actually recorded in the diary that I still loved Margaret and wanted to respond to her. Yet, once everything was out in the open, and I had time to think more about it, there was no doubt in my mind that I hankered after Maggie. A diary entry made on 10th November, just after I'd resigned from the church reads: "I desire to begin life again with another who loves me. The prospect looks remote, but I hope against hope to win her one day. I want a good well-paid job... I want to enjoy music, the theatre, books, walking."

One Sunday morning, when I decided to stay at home, rather than go to church, I took it as an opportunity to face up to my questioning and doubting God. Having struggled to hold on to Christianity, partly for the sake of my congregation, I now felt no obligation to do so. The question I asked myself was why I should continue to give credence to beliefs that I've frequently questioned or even temporarily abandoned. At this time, I decisively opted for atheism.

John M Hayes

Diary Entry: 24th October 1980

"How free I now feel! For the first time in nineteen years, I'm free to pursue life away from the spotlight. How refreshing it will be, sitting on the back benches... Best of all an opportunity has been provided for me to carve out a new career, in the 'real' world. So far, I have applied for the post office. For a while, it may be necessary to take a postman's job, but eventually, I want to get something much better than that."

The last sentence of this extract is, I believe, so important because it partly defines me and explains, why I did eventually find a satisfying and lucrative career. The sentence is 'ambition will drive me on.' Here it is again—'wanting to be different.'

My resignation from the Pastorate came within days of the Deacons meeting me. Another diary entry, made a fortnight later, reveals how my thinking had so quickly moved on.

Diary Entry: 10th November 1980

"Since resigning from the Pastorate, I've tried to find myself and decide what I really want.

First of all, I am now an atheist. There is no God! What a relief not to be pressurised to fight for a faith."

The next thing was to find a job. Fortunately, the post office in Amersham was always short of staff, so it was easy to obtain employment there. It kept me going for six months. In some ways, the job was enjoyable and rewarding but a six-day week of early starts meant that one was hardly ever fully awake! At first, I delivered locally on a bicycle, but, fairly soon, graduated to delivering in a van on four different country routes—that is one of the things I enjoyed. I saw some lovely countryside as well as some fabulous houses. (I felt envious then but not in my wildest dreams I'd imagined that one day I'd be living in such a house.)

One of the difficult things about abandoning the church was the loss of friends. One or two people, however, stood by us, especially the remarkable Ray and Barbara Eyres. For the first time ever, Margaret and I could now attend classical music concerts in London. With Ray and Barbara, we booked a series in the Royal Festival Hall. I relished it.

In the Spring of 1981, walking around the lanes near Chesham, I suddenly felt that I must, again, give some credence to religion. I had missed all the positive things that it gives—a sense of purpose, especially. After some thought, although my theology was now extremely vague, I thought it worth exploring the ministry in the Church of England. Robin Smith, my old friend, provided an introduction to the Bishop of Buckingham. The interview resulted in the bishop wisely saying that he could not recommend me for Ordination. By then, I'd left the post office and was, half-heartedly, trying to sell various kinds of insurance for Manulife from their office in Oxford. The bishop told me to get on with my insurance job! But after three months, and after forming a negative view of the industry, I left. About the same time, though, I joined the Church of England, even being confirmed by the bishop. Chenies Parish Church, and its mission church in Little Chalfont, had an easy-going, totally undogmatic vicar. He encouraged me to engage in pastoral work, and even take the odd service. There were some lovely men there, generally, highly intelligent and quite well-off, and I made friends. One chap I got close to was a retired army Major whose motto in life was 'Everything in excess.' I shall never forget one evening, in my house, he must have imbibed a third of a bottle of whisky before getting into his car to drive off. He was a very genuine, warm-hearted man. By this time, we had bought a modern house (not very well-built) in Little Chalfont, following just a short time living in an Amersham flat.

After three months, I left the insurance industry, believing it to be highly corrupt. To this day, I don't have a lot of respect for it, although it must be said we have a very good service from 'The Liverpool and Victoria'—a mutual insurance company. For work, which was so essential to keep me occupied, I took a job in a local petrol station. For £80.00 per week, I worked in the open for ten hours a day, five days a week, from Monday to Friday, filling cars with petrol. Not very stimulating, but I was kept busy, not even having time-off for a lunch hour! One thing this showed about me—I must have something to do, and I'm not too proud to take a dirty job!

In time, vague thoughts occurred about a possible return to Baptist ministry. Incredibly, Hugh Logan, the area superintendent, encouraged me; he promised to try and find me a church. In the Autumn of 1981, Hugh mentioned one or two openings but, finally, in 1982, he took me for an interview to Wellingborough Baptist Church. Amazingly, just at this time, something else had turned up on the scene—a career as a Law Costs Draftsman. Like, perhaps, most people, I'd never heard of it. Margaret, however, taught the children of a man, Philip Rigby, who did this work. One day, he said that if I were interested, he would take me on to train. Torn between this offer and the possibility of going to Wellingborough, I decided that if Wellingborough decided to invite me, I'd go, but if they didn't, I would give up the church idea altogether and start work as a Trainee Costs Draftsman. The latter thing happened. Thank goodness! Another start as a Baptist Minister would have turned into a disaster. My beliefs had become so vague; the church would have soon got rid of me! Phew! What an embarrassing and destructive situation that would have been!

Whoever has read the last paragraph, or two, must be feeling rather confused. How could I, having turned from faith to faithless, have possibly considered going back into the church? Actually, I was in denial. What I continued to hanker for was some vague 'spirituality.' At the time, a new movement in the Church of England rejected the traditional creeds. The doctrine of the Holy Trinity was 'spurned' in favour of 'The Ground of our Being.' Out of this arose 'The Sea of Faith' movement. It was something like this to which I was feeling attracted. In other words, everything was symbolic, even the idea of God itself. So, it was possible to participate in a church service without believing, literally, in anything!

There was also another pull. My pastoral and counselling work had, over the years, provided huge fulfilment to me. It would be wonderful if this ministry could be revived.

To me, at this time, perhaps, the words of George Eliott would have made sense.

"Not God is love, but love is God."

An attendance at a Spinners concert, just before Christmas 1981, evoked such thoughts.

Diary Entry: 20th December 1981

"We went to a Spinners concert in the Fulcrum Centre, Slough…

Whether or not any of the lads are religious, I found the concert a deeply moving occasion. It wasn't the carols which evoked a religious response, but the general demeanour of the group. They came across as such genuine people, standing by the values of Christmas. The singing evoked feelings of brotherliness, warmth, gentleness, kindness, wonder."

So, I clung on to the church attendance for some time, before finally, in 1986, it became clear that I couldn't both have my cake and eat it.

At this point, in the narrative, it seems appropriate to explain more about my faith pilgrimage from sixteen to forty-six. What caused me to slowly lose a vibrant faith and why did the process take so long? It isn't easy to say how and why, but the attempt will be made.

John M Hayes

Chapter Ten
FROM FAITH TO FAITHLESS

My original 'born again' beliefs were based on the Bible. My peer group were adamant—the Bible was the Word of God, every word of it! At first, the joy of the conversion experience carried me along with this view. Me, being me, however, this couldn't last! I didn't know much about science, but like almost everyone, I'd heard of Darwin! To take the creation story in the Book of Genesis literally, was more than I could swallow. (The trouble is, as my best college friend, Peter Edwards, used to say: "If one begins questioning something in the Bible, one is on a slippery slope.")

Until the time I spent at Glasgow Bible College, the fundamentalist view of the Bible generally held.

Through more intensive study, however, I gradually moved to a less literalist position. One day, the strictest fundamentalist tutor in the college announced he was to give a special lecture. His project was to attempt a reconciliation of some of the 'apparent' discrepancies in part of the Old Testament. As an old Etonian, he deserved respect, but for me, his lecture was totally unconvincing. His reasoning came across as special pleading.

So, I had very slightly come to move away from my early 'conversion' views. Yet, this move didn't, even in the slightest, undermine my faith.

What happened one day, in private though, was another matter. The story has already been related. It was the day, when saying my prayers, the involuntary thought came into my head: "I wonder if I'm just talking to the ceiling?" This came as a shock. My thought was suggesting that there might not even be a God!

Wherever had the thought come from? It must have come from my subconscious. Of course, I ferociously squashed it at the time. But it was impossible to deny that it had occurred, and its force was such that I couldn't ever forget it. So, what do I think brought on this question?

Perhaps, experiencing life in the Gorbals slums had some influence. Although I tried my best to bring the gospel to the people, it would now seem that, subconsciously, I thought the message seemed of no relevance to these people, to the actual lives they were living. Was it not significant that after two years of evangelising not one convert was made? The claim that without being 'saved' by Christ, a person had no purpose, and that beyond death, they were going to Hell, became a very difficult position to hold. Besides anything else, this belief seemed to be a contradiction of the notion of a loving God!

The idea of Hell became unpalatable to me. (It also disturbed me that none of my family were believers. So, what was their fate going to be?)

Another thing that knocked my faith was the emotionally dependent relationship with Elaine Berry, the student who helped me with New Testament Greek, in connection with the proposed application to Spurgeon's College. This created confusion and insecurity, and, naturally, had a negative effect on my feelings for Margaret, my wife. All of this inevitably led to a slackening of confidence in my Christian beliefs. Again, it was mostly subconscious, though.

Surely, the decisions we make about what to believe are not entirely based on reason; the emotions also play a part. There is such a thing as 'emotional intelligence.' So it was, I think, that some of my strong convictions were undermined.

The one period of my life when firm beliefs were recovered was in the late sixties, following some intensive counselling. (I've already written about this.) What happened at this time was that my emotional life became more stable. This more settled state, however, didn't last. Deep-rooted things had not been completely removed.

What I'm saying is that when people abandon 'the faith,' it is, probably, never for intellectual reasons alone. The happenings in their personal life, in their relationships, are profoundly significant. This is difficult to convey in words, but it is very real, and certainly was for me.

(It should surprise no one that the catalyst that led to my abandoning the ministry in the church and declaring myself to be an atheist was the affair with Maggie in 1980.)

Moving on now to the four years in Spurgeon's College. The excitement of moving on to study for a degree, temporarily covered up any questions and doubts. Nevertheless, whilst there, I was tempted to abandon 'the faith' on more than one occasion. Once again, this happened through a combination of intellectual questioning and personal suffering.

Educationally, Spurgeon's was more than a step-up from the Bible College; the main studies were related to a London University Degree in Divinity.

Throughout one's studies, it was impossible to escape the common questions about religious faith. Why didn't God create a less cruel world? Why does he allow so much suffering to persist? Why doesn't he make himself more obvious to people? Why should the Bible be believed any more, or less, than the Koran or the sacred texts of the other numerous religions?

The philosophical questioning came thick and fast, yet questions remained unanswered. One tended to suppress the questioning, not relishing facing up to issues. If one talks to any practicing Christian about 'doubt,' they'll often say, "Yes, we all have doubts." Yes, but what do we do about it? Usually, and this is what I tried to do, we simply put our head in the sand and stubbornly refuse to allow our faith to be shaken. That is what I did, but then in 1965, a family tragedy changed me.

The college term had just begun in September. Before setting out for college, I was having breakfast, when the doorbell rang. My wife responded. She brought in a telegram—it reported that my dad had been rushed into hospital and had quite suddenly died. Once again, this had been written about previously. Here, I need to elaborate on how the sudden death of dad, at forty-six, affected my faith, not just immediately, but for many years thereafter.

Within weeks, bitterness took over. Sadly, not one of the college faculty asked about my dad or sought to support me in any way. It was almost unbelievable—here were men training others to be what were often called pastors! They certainly failed in their pastoral care of me, and other students, I may add. Unfortunately, I turned against them, called them 'hypocrites,' and that led to turning against what they represented—God!

Apparently, it has often been the case that people abandon their beliefs on suffering a bereavement. Logically, it perhaps doesn't make sense, but as I've just written, it's the emotions, not logic that comes into it sometimes.

For a time, as I told Margaret, I would stay in college, take the degree, then try to find a job teaching Religious Education.

The trouble is, I again sorely missed my faith and almost forced myself to believe again. So much had been invested; how could I just let it all slip through my fingers? So, throughout these college years, there was a constant battle going on; I so much wanted to believe, yet, frequently, found myself questioning, sometimes doubting. One thing is certain, I was not a happy man.

The degree course was completed, and I passed. This gave me another lift. By then, I was on the way to being a minister in the Doncaster church. Once there, I somehow managed to get by, for a while. The first four years, however, were quite stressful at times. I continued to wrestle with the now long-standing issues, including a sense of disappointment with my marriage and, of course, the resulting guilt!

Then came a temporary respite. Counselling received on a special week's retreat dispersed some of the anger, bitterness and guilt. On returning home, I discovered a new freedom, domestically and professionally. No wonder people almost lined up at my study door in the hope of receiving the help that I'd personally benefitted from.

The irony is that, in time, this fulfilling work itself led to more questioning. Although participants gave God the credit for any improvement in their lives, I began to think otherwise. Was any 'healing' due to divine intervention or was it simply a thoroughly human process? Some of the techniques used were, clearly, taken from 'secular' counselling and psychiatry. Gradually, as more people passed through the study door, I wondered if any success was actually due, in large part at least, to the fact that the counsellors were prepared to really listen, and to go on listening for as long as necessary—as well as being non-judgemental. This was the position I'd adopted, by the time, I was about to take a sabbatical, before moving to my second church.

It has already been mentioned that, for my ten weeks in Oxford, I had chosen to study the theologian Paul Tillich, an American whom evangelicals insisted was not really a Christian! Some of my friends were surprised at my choice but most of them were quite unaware of my inner questioning and confusion.

In December 1974, I was inducted to the Pastorate of Trinity Baptist Church in Chesham. Almost from day one, I felt unhappy, and often felt lonely. Again, the lack of intimacy, other than sexual, with Margaret perpetuated this state of affairs. (I must emphasise that I'm not blaming her for anything but simply saying how it was.) I'd lost the support group of Doncaster, which led to a feeling of isolation. Troubles arose in the church, with growing attacks on me from the more traditional church members. Then, in my immaturity and insecurity, I exacerbated matters by becoming angry and judgemental. My pleadings to God for forgiveness as well as for him to make me a better man were unheeded, which, again, caused me to imagine he may not be there! Undoubtedly, a part of my toying with atheism, time and time again, was because prayers for help didn't make a scrap of difference. As I've often told people in later life, "I was always looking for God, but never found him!"

It's like the true story of a Jewish man who survived a Nazi Death Camp. When asked if his faith in God helped him, he cooly replied, "God wasn't there!"

Earlier, I've recorded the story of how the church, being so divided, eventually split. On the one hand, this took the pressure off me; a cynic would say the congregation now consisted of 'yes men.' On the other hand, I felt quite guilty how could a split church be an effective advertisement for the Christian faith, which is supposed to be about 'loving God and loving your neighbour as yourself?' Again, things were not working out as one would have expected!

Depression, loneliness and sadness were now compounded with a shortage of work. Time on my hands was unhealthy. It meant that when Maggie and I fell in love there was plenty of opportunity to meet, or just speak on the telephone. How I carried on for about four months still conducting services and trying to continue with pastoral work, I really don't know. But I was actually heading for a breakdown. Even at the time, I suspected this, the quality of my preaching deteriorated markedly. Of course, the conviction had gone, and it showed.

Perhaps, it was fortuitous that the matter was taken out of my hands. We were found out. Then, on being given the opportunity to have as much time off as required, I only felt relief. Maggie and I could hardly continue to meet. In fact, we decided that we must remain with our families. Maggie couldn't abandon her children.

Within no time at all, I felt free from the pressure to avoid facing the facts. The facts were that I had lost religious convictions some time ago. Now, I no longer had to consider responsibility for a congregation. This situation was the catalyst that gave me the courage to, finally, renounce former beliefs and accept there were no Gods; I had adopted atheism. The relief at that moment was amazing. I felt a huge burden had been lifted. I felt free to enjoy all the little joys of life and not to take life so desperately seriously.

Although Maggie and I denied ourselves, at this time, I had no regrets at what we did, for it had, indirectly, led to my freedom from years of turmoil. The door opened onto an amazingly interesting and enjoyable life. But it took time to come to fruition.

Chapter Eleven
THE PURPOSE OF LIFE IS TO ENJOY BEING ALIVE

The story, so far, has taken us to 1982; I was then forty-two, halfway through my life. The second part of my life may be covered in a second volume, rather than in this one.

Significant developments, however, relating to the 'faith to faithless' theme, took place in these later years, so they are included here.

Having abandoned faith and settled for atheism, I was left with a philosophical and emotional emptiness (Atheism, after all, only indicates what one isn't, that is one doesn't believe in the existence of Gods, rather than what one is!). Ultimately, the 'hole' was filled by what may be called 'humanism,' but I came to this position well before discovering the modern humanist movement itself.

This is a long story, and I need to provide here a context, that is, to write about what happened in my life during these years from 1982. Here then is an outline.

In June 1982, I embarked on a career as a Law Costs Draftsman, working for one Philip Rigby. Little did I realise, at the time, how this move would lay the foundation of a nationwide business of my own. At Rigby's, the work proved to be interesting, the money excellent, yet, after two and a half years, I left. Rigby had never once thanked me for the work I'd done, and the atmosphere in the office was toxic! In January 1985, I set up as a sole practitioner working from our dining room. (By now, between us, we were earning good money. This had enabled the purchase of a fairly new four-bedroomed house in Amersham-on-the-Hill.)

I was never one for allowing work to take over completely, and even though work inevitably occupied much of my time, I also gave serious attention to politics. Since 1981, I enjoyed membership of the Labour Party, and this was the beginning of twenty-five years of engagement (though I resigned and rejoined twice in that time!) Never one for half-hearted involvement, I assumed official responsibilities, especially as Treasurer of the Chesham and Amersham Parliamentary Constituency Labour Pary. Perhaps, more significantly and, certainly for me, more interestingly, from 1984, I became involved with the party at the national level. This provided me with the stimulating opportunity to meet politicians such as Robin Cook and Gordon Brown, among many others. Once I'd joined 'The Smith Institute,' one of Gordon Brown's creations, I frequently attended meetings in 11 Downing Street. This gave me a sense of purpose; in a very small way, I felt able to contribute to discussions on 'policy.' I had arrived on the national stage

By 1986, hankering to return to our roots, Margaret and I decided to look for a house in Derbyshire. We found one in Matlock and moved in at the very end of 1986. A friend I'd met during my post office days, a Jeff Paget, had, by then, been working with me for well over a year; he was appointed manager in Amersham.

One reason for moving to Matlock was to give a boost to our faltering marriage; after all, it was in Matlock that I'd proposed to Margaret, and it had been accepted. Yes, even after all the failings, we were still trying! At the time, I believed the move would help me to emotionally break with Maggie and, in any case, I still felt a lot for Margaret, despite everything!

Sadly, within just days of arriving in 'The Garden House,' my hopes were dashed and my intentions thwarted. Once Margaret had grasped that I wasn't going to attend church anymore, she became very upset. "Our marriage can never be the same again!" she exclaimed. This really threw me. Unsurprisingly, I later began to doubt whether we would stay together after all.

Whilst in Matlock, a viable second office of the business was established, quite quickly. Within three years, however, I felt obliged to return south. Jeff Paget, having problems in the office, expressed the opinion that I should resume responsibility. In 1990, this is what happened.

Margaret found a house, 'The Galway' in Chesham Bois, which adjoins Amersham.

In the meantime, Andrea North assumed responsibility for Matlock. (She later became the first general manager for the business.) Also in 1990, Jeff Paget opened our Yorkshire office whilst Harry Birks, from the Matlock team, opened an office in Birmingham. All this hectic activity arose out of a driving ambition—I wanted a nationwide business. Growing this business was proving to be so exciting as well as financially rewarding. (The income was completely enhancing my lifestyle! Good clothes, eating in excellent restaurants, buying very good wines, taking exciting holidays, buying more expensive homes and cars, as well as using 'spare' money to assist family members and charities. This way of life stood in marked contrast to life in the church!)

On returning to Amersham, I threw myself, even more, into politics. Being so close to London, once again, meant that I could do this without any need to have expensive overnight stays.

So, life was full and exciting. On reaching fifty, however, I began seriously to question whether staying with Margaret was the right thing to do. Neither of us were happy with our relationship, and there was a danger of us creeping into a bitter old age. Yet, it took another two years of ambivalent feelings before a final decision was made. In 1992, I resolved to leave Margaret; at the time, even she thought that having some time apart may be beneficial. Whilst all this was in the air, I began wondering about where Maggie was. If Margaret and I were to separate, would it be worth finding out whether Maggie still had any feelings for me? Having lost touch with her, I instructed a private investigator to find her. He came up with the goods! Having obtained details of her whereabouts and employment, I turned up at a bus stop at 7.15 a.m. to offer a lift to work. Almost immediately, after accepting the invitation, she told me that more than once she had said to her flatmate, "One of these days, John will turn up at the bottom of our road looking for me." Well, the rest, as they say, is history.

On Boxing Day 1992, I moved into Hartwell House Hotel but, within weeks, bought a newly built house, 4 Pump Meadow, Great Missenden. Maggie, for the time being, continued to live in a council flat, which had been found for her. Naturally, however, we spent a lot of time together.

Then, out of the blue, a letter came through the door. It was from a local widow. She wanted to buy my house! The timing was perfect as only recently we had made the decision to move to Derbyshire. (By now, Maggie herself was just beginning to share my appreciation of the county, having spent time there on holiday with me. We were now engaged to be married (This had taken place in the county whilst we were staying at Fischers in Baslow.). In August 1994, we moved into 'Highbury' in Grindleford, or I did; Maggie followed some weeks later. We were now, officially, a couple.

Although we came to love the house as well as the area, just under five years later, we bought a larger house. (We now had not only seven children, some with partners, but also several grandchildren—we needed something larger than the three-bedroomed 'Highbury.')

In 1999, we settled into a former Georgian Rectory, with an acre of garden. It was situated in Old Brampton, a small village that I'd known and liked since the 1950s. I was, immediately, so impressed that before long I could be heard exclaiming "I'll never leave here!" That same year we were married at a ceremony in Fischers. We were both fifty-nine, but we felt like forty-year-olds! ('Life begins at forty!') Certainly, we felt so settled, happy and fulfilled. The Old Rectory was then our home for twenty-one years.

So, we were now fully established and comfortable, both in marriage and employment.

Now, I come to the main subject for this chapter that is to relate how the 'gap' left by the abandonment of religion was, finally, filled. It was a very gradual process, but I did begin to find some sense of purpose again, quite soon. One could describe it as a road that led to my adoption of a humanist approach to life, though the UK Humanist movement was unknown to me before 2009!

Throughout my life, the natural world had always fascinated me. I came to appreciate it, especially when going for walks. After leaving the church, I had more spare time to enjoy it. Since childhood, I'd spent time birdwatching, and though not very good at it, I now took this more seriously. It encouraged me that Maggie also began to show an interest. Walking together, enjoying landscape and wildlife, increasingly became an essential aspect of our lives.

In the years covered in this chapter, there are hundreds of references in my diary as to the significance of the natural world in my life. I was discovering that engaging with nature was making me feel whole again. At the risk of confusing the reader, I could say that the 'natural' was now providing me with something of a 'spiritual' experience. (Throughout history, many others have spoken about this from their own experience.)

My granddaughter, Aimée, bought me a book, 'The Old Ways: A Journey on Foot' by Robert Macfarlane. A sentence that occurs early in the book resonated with me. He's writing about walking: "To go out, is to go in." I instantly understood what Macfarlane meant.

From the huge number of diary entries on this subject, I'm including here, perhaps, the best example, which was written on my birthday in 2005 (age sixty-five).

Diary Entry: 18th February 2005

"At 5 o'clock, the sun is still shining. It is such a contrast to this morning. I, especially, appreciated the atmosphere on the moor, created by the mist, wintry rain and strong winds... Going back to this morning's walk, we saw the most fabulous rainbow. Rainbows are, usually ephemeral, but this one lasted for ages... To see such a sight, a great symbol of hope on my sixty-fifth birthday, was fantastic!

John M Hayes

.... All my life, even today on Froggatt, nature has given me so much pleasure, a sense of wholeness, peace, certainly a sense of belonging."

I then go on to quote both William Wordsworth and Walt Whitman.

Diary Entry: 18th February 2005
"Nature never did betray the heart that loved her" – Wordsworth. This was followed by Walt Whitman – "After you have exhausted what there is in business, politics, conviviality and so on, what remains? Nature remains."

Another phenomenon that provided a similar gift to nature, was music, especially classical music. Throughout adult life, I had listened to radio programmes such as 'Your Favourite 100 Tunes' but couldn't afford any musical equipment or records. In 1985, however, I acquired some excellent second-hand Linn Sondek and, immediately, went into a record-buying frenzy. (Someone in the Chesham church had lent me some equipment and a few records previously, and I had come to love Beethoven.) Now, I discovered many more composers. The Russians, Tchaikovsky and Rachmaninov, remained favourites, but it was a joy to discover Sibelius and Bruckner, for instance.

Listening to music together with walking became a main occupation in my leisure time. A love affair developed with the BBC Proms. Every year, I attended some concerts live and also listened to some recordings on the television. Following the move to Derbyshire, we regularly attended Sheffield City Hall Concerts. As with the engagement with nature, there are also hundreds of references in my diary to music. I recorded that music too gave me a sense of transcendence—yes, something like the 'spiritual.' Music provided joy, comfort, and a sense of being taken 'out of this world,' with all its troubles.

Ten years after I'd left the church, it is clear from consulting my diary that listening to music was one of the things that was helping me recover from my loss.

A QUEST FOR MEANING: A Memoir from Pit to Pulpit; from Business to Philanthropy

Diary Entry: 11th October 1990

"An evening at home on my own, listening to music. To begin with, Britten's War Requiem, marvellous, but too intellectually demanding for me tonight, followed by Tchaikovsky's 5th. Oh, what glorious music. His theme, that destiny cannot be evaded, but that one can deliberately embrace it and, in a sense, live triumphantly with it, (or something like that), really strikes home to me. And now, the brilliant, triumphant sound of Beethoven's 5th are ringing in my ears.

What more could I ask from life?!"

This extract reveals the intensity of my involvement with music. The written comments also suggest that music was supplying me with much of the emotional and intellectual content that 'faith' had at one time provided. More than once, this point was reiterated in the diaries. I will continue with the diary entry just quoted.

Diary Entry: 11th October 1990

"Still listening to Beethoven. His 5th and Tchaikovsky's 5th have a profound, personal meaning for me. The symphonies are more than mere favourites; they speak to the ground of my being, and give expression to true emotions. They inspire courage, determination and joy as nothing else does."

A third activity also helped me to find 'wholeness' again—reading. Whilst in the church, I had spent much of the mornings reading; the books though were confined, largely, to the Bible and volumes of theology. In my subject, I became widely read. Of course, some novels and other books on general topics were read, but in the religious phase of my existence, my connection with literature was primarily with religious subjects. (I read the Bible daily and, unsurprisingly, became able to quote large chunks of it, by heart.) Then in 1981, most of the books I had were sold to students at Spurgeon's College. At last, I began to read more generally. Throughout the following years, I became a voracious reader, and this, unsurprisingly, helped in the development of my ideas about life.

Apart from reading some of the classics (Thomas Hardy became a favourite), I generally read biographies, autobiographies and history. My interest was, and remains, with real life (far more exciting than any fiction)!

People increasingly fascinated me. It was through reading that some humanist ideas began to be formed in me. Reading about the lives of others gave me a fuller appreciation of human capabilities, a deeper awareness of what life is, or could be. Scores of volumes were purchased, read and digested. At times, I noted in the diary the books being read; sometimes, the list was long. Often, when browsing in a bookshop, particularly a second-hand one, I noticed a book that though unfamiliar to me looked interesting, and I bought it. Quite a few of these acquisitions turned out to be significant in the development of my philosophy of living. One indication of the effect that reading had on me can be illustrated by my habit of noting down quotations from the books being read. This is a practice begun before I left the church. Eventually, I filled several substantial notebooks. (I often quote some of these in conversation and repeat them in any talks or speeches I make.) To me, these quotations became my treasure box of wisdom—they provide something of a guide to living. They provide something like an outline-philosophy, suggestions, if you like, on how to live.

To give some idea of the flavour of the books being read, I'll quote from a diary entry of 1998.

Diary Entry:
- *"Growing Up in the Gorbals – Ralph Glasser (three volumes)*
- *Biography of Charles Darwin – Juliet Ackroyd*
- *An Evil Cradling – Brian Keenan*
- *Portrait of the Artist as a Young Man – James Joyce*
- *The Scarlett Letter – Nathaniel Hawthorne*
- *The Pickwick Papers – Charles Dickens*
- *Biography of Gerard Manley Hopkins*

A QUEST FOR MEANING: A Memoir from Pit to Pulpit; from Business to Philanthropy

- *Poetry of Gerard Manley Hopkins*
- *The Heart of Darkness – Joseph Conrad*
- *Sarah Miles (two volumes biography)*
- *Measure for Measure – William Shakespeare*
- *The Mayor of Casterbridge – Thomas Hardy*
- *Some natural history books:*
- *Tropic of Capricorn – Henry Miller*
- *Damned to Fame (biography of Samuel Beckett) – James Knowlson*
- *The Land is Our Land – Marion Shoard*
- *My Traitor's Heart – Rian Malan*
- *Brideshead Revisited – Evelyn Waugh*
- *First Love – Ivan Turgenev*
- *Clinging to the Wreckage: A Part of Life – John Mortimer*
- *The Road to Wigan Pier – George Orwell*
- *The Rise and Fall of the Third Reich (three volumes) – William L Shirer*
- *Life Without Armour – Alan Sillitoe*
- *In Defence of Sensuality – John Cowper Powys*
- *On Philosophy and Essays – Isaiah Berlin*
- *Swinburnes Poetry (two volumes) – Algernon Charles Swinburne*

All of these books were read between 1994 and 1998. The list is not comprehensive, but it illustrates my preference for 'serious' literature!

In later diaries, I made similar lists of my reading. (I was determined to make up for lost time!) Maggie now tells me that she thinks I'm well-read! If this is so, it is surely only in the genre of biography and autobiography and Victorian history. There is no doubt people fascinate me, and I've learned so much from reading about people whose lives have been different from my own.

This reference to 'people' brings me to the third great influence on my philosophical and emotional development—relationships. Increasingly, I came to appreciate the crucial importance of engaging with people. Even casual encounters were, sometimes, enriching. My diary is saturated with incidents of this, as well as reflections on friendships formed. Maggie played a big part in this. Each of us had come to miss the church 'community' where friendships had been enjoyed. (Each of us, by abandoning the church, had lost these friends and acquaintances, and we felt the loss deeply.) Not surprisingly, we made determined efforts to engage with neighbours and others. (We were fortunate to have quite a large family too.) Maggie, like me, through having a leadership role in the church, quite naturally reached out to people. We became an enthusiastic partnership. People were invited to enjoy our hospitality and a few reciprocated. Before long, we made new friends. To paraphrase Bertrand Russell, "The secret of happiness is to have lots of interests and many friends and acquaintances."

Well, by the late 1990s, I had nurtured interests, found new friends but also enjoyed innumerable casual encounters that brought a sense of life being worthwhile.

When visiting one of our offices, I increasingly chose to travel by train. Of these hundreds of journeys, there must be a very few where I didn't benefit from a casual conversation. Many of these encounters were recorded in the diary. On arriving home from a journey, I frequently couldn't contain my excitement and immediately had to pour out the story to Maggie. The intensity of my enthusiasm was a clear indication of how much had been gained from these casual encounters. People were sharing their lives with me; I was learning so much about what life is all about, and I was all the time, growing in confidence as people, through showing interest, affirmed me.

In my pilgrimage from 'faith to faithless' and to humanism, 2006 was a pivotal year. I spent a few days in a York hotel on a personal retreat. On going into a city's second-hand bookshop, I saw a copy of An Atheist's Values by an Oxford Don, Richard Richardson. I had found an author who, though an atheist, expounded a profoundly fulfilling way to live—a life full of purpose and joy. On reading one of his quotations from a person called Skeaping, I immediately identified with it. "The purpose of life is to enjoy being alive." That was it; that's what I had, finally, realised. I was now very much enjoying being alive. My life was full of interests and activities; I had a family, friends and a whole host of acquaintances. Altogether, my life was full and overflowing! The stifling pressure of religion had been replaced by 'life more abundant.' After reading An Atheist's Values, I felt like dancing for joy! Maggie and I were now enthusiastically enjoying so much, family, the natural world, serious walks, music, books and a wide circle of people. It is worth mentioning that, by now, we had also discovered and, fallen in love with Italy and the Italians who appeared to emphasise 'enjoying life.' Italian culture, sculpture, painting and architecture. Quite a few pieces of art were to eventually grace our home, mainly the work of artists we'd met.

Speaking of enjoying life, a conversation I had with an Irish woman living near Siena is worth quoting. The woman was managing a holiday property we used for several years. She told me of the 'horrors' of being brought up in Catholic Ireland when children were often made to feel excessive guilt. But she went on to say, "The Italians are just as religious, but without the guilt!"

After some years, learning more of Florence being a centre of the Renaissance, I realise it was this that probably, developed the zest for life! Some scholars refer to some of the leading thinkers of that time as being 'humanist.' Though still religious, they had rediscovered from the classical world, the joy of life in the here and now. They valued life on earth and some, like the Epicureans, emphasised the pleasures that are available to all, good food and drink, for instance!

So, it was that I began to see that the purpose of life, if there was one at all, was to make the most of it! My position may be summed up in the words of a Victorian American, Robert G Ingersol, an agnostic and rationalist. (Some recordings made by him in 1899 are preserved in a museum in his birthplace, Dresden, New York.) Here is an extract:

"Is life worth living? Well, I can only answer for myself. I like to be alive, to breathe the air, to look at the landscape, the clouds, the stars, to repeat old poems, to look at pictures and statues, to hear music, the voices of the ones I love. I enjoy eating and smoking. I like good cold water. I like to talk with my wife, my girls, my grandchildren. I like to sleep and to dream. Yes, you can say that life, to me, is worth living."

Twenty-five years then after abandoning 'faith,' I was enjoying what one can say is a humanist approach to living. This was well before I had heard of The British Humanist Association (now, Humanists UK).

In 2009, however, the association ran a campaign, advertising on London's red buses; it was a slogan:

"THERE'S PROBABLY NO GOD. NOW STOP WORRYING AND ENJOY YOUR LIFE."

Having heard of this campaign, I decided to find out more. Within no time at all, I joined the association, then gradually became quite involved. Apart from attendance at two annual meetings, my primary involvement was to make donations towards campaigns such as the one advocating support for assisted dying, or for better control of or even the banning of faith schools.

My engagement deepened a few years later by joining the Blackham Society. The membership of this group was quite exclusive; members were expected to regularly contribute significant amounts of money to Humanists UK. The group meets about four times a year. I participate whenever possible, and to my delight, Maggie often accompanies me as my guest! It has been a privilege to get to know Andrew Copson, the chief executive, as well as several presidents, particularly, Jim Al Khalili, the physicist, and employees of Humanists UK.

For some years, the organisation has authorised some members to become 'school volunteers,' and this is a route I decided to take. On 25th March 2017, I attended a 'school volunteer training programme.' It was months before my first engagement came along, but it was a marvellous one when it did come. The Southall Minster Academy arranged for a panel of speakers to speak on three subjects, two of which were 'abortion' and 'assisted dying.' My contribution went down well with most of the teachers approaching me to express appreciation. And this was in a C of E school! The following year, I was invited back! Since then, I've spoken in a Roman Catholic Academy (twice); a local junior school (an all-day appointment); another local junior school (twice); a junior school in Retford (twice); a large academy in Eastwood; DH Lawrence's birthplace (over two days, once on a panel and once in the lecture hall, for a solo appearance); and even, amazingly, an infant school in Nottingham!

Although it has meant only two or three visits in a year, I've learnt a lot through having to prepare. Of course, a fresh approach is taken with each appointment, but, somehow, I try to convey three key elements of a humanist approach to life; they are:

- Freedom of thought, speech and action
- Enjoyment—the importance of developing interests to enjoy
- Caring (or kindness)—happiness comes not only by enjoying oneself but by engaging with other people and taking an interest in them

Personally, I dislike to use the term 'humanism,' but I'm more comfortable alluding to 'a humanist approach to life.' Each individual must interpret what that means for them. As I'm writing about my own life, let me say how I would sum it up. If asked to explain in a sentence what is the essence of a humanist approach to life, my answer would be: "Being enthusiastic and passionate about life." Anyone who has read this account, so far, will not be surprised by this declaration. Of course, it is, partly, about personality and not simply a lifestyle choice. My natural personality is, shall we say, more ebullient than most people. On once reading the novel Howard's End, I quickly identified with the character 'Margaret.' To quote: "She had a profound vivacity and a sincere and continual interest in all that she encountered in her path through life." On reading this, I noted in my diary:

Diary Entry: 9th July 2017

"Perhaps, this is what people are sometimes spotting in me; people like Ron Enock, for instance, who makes me feel 'interesting' for being so alive

to things, so enthusiastic... Interestingly, it is something similar which draws people to Maggie and causes them to comment on it!"

It must be said, to be balanced in this, that a person like the character in the book can be a 'pain in the neck' by their extreme effusiveness; I'm certainly aware that I sometimes go 'over the top!' But the passion, the enthusiasm is genuine. Another person I closely identify with, and this time, it is a living, real human being, David Hockney. He has often spoken of the joy he finds in the natural world, for instance; I once read that he even found joy in 'splashing through a puddle of water on a Bridlington pavement.' Here is enthusiasm for life! Maggie's daughter, Angela, sent me a birthday card in 2022. On the front was printed "SOME PEOPLE WHILST LOOKING FOR SOME BIG THING, MISS ALL THE LITTLE JOYS OF LIFE." Inside the card, Angela has written:

"John…
Whereas you take every joy from life."

www.ingramcontent.com/pod-product-compliance
Lightning Source LLC
Chambersburg PA
CBHW052033070526
44584CB00016B/2029